LAST OF THE SAILORMEN

Last of the Sailormen

by

BOB ROBERTS

SEAFARER BOOKS
LONDON

First published in 1960
Reprinted in this edition by
Seafarer Books
3 Manchester Road
London E14 9BD

© *Bob Roberts 1960, 1986*

British Library Cataloguing in Publication Data

Roberts, Rob, *1907-1982*
    Last of the sailormen.
    1. Coastwise shipping——England
    I. Title
    387.5'092'4   HE826

ISBN 0-85036-342-X

Printed in Great Britain by
Whitstable Litho Ltd., Whitstable, Kent

'Gone all those beautiful vessels and every man of their crews—and the world is the worse for it.'

Contents

Illustrations

Sketches by Anne Roberts

Photographs

Preface

—————— ❋ ——————

MUCH of this book has been written in a barge's cabin, rolling at anchor in Yarmouth Roads, storm-bound under the lee of the Yantlet Flats, waiting to load at Keadby or while lying idle in London River. I have not attempted to glorify or exaggerate this account of life in a type of sailing craft which is one of the most unique and efficient in the world. It is a life in which, to my mind, the pleasantness, satisfaction and occasional thrills, calling for the exercise of a man's more sterling qualities, far outweigh the times of hardship and frustration.

Sailing barges, like farm horses, belonged to a more peaceful and expansive age than the uncertain, war-wracked, nervy, money-grubbing years to which mankind has descended. A bargeman knows nothing of regular working hours, overtime pay, crowded city trains, noisy, bustling streets, or the clanging hell of a vast, modern factory. Like the fisherman, the wildfowler, and the farm hand, he lives by the winds and the weather, the tides and the seasons. The artificial sort of life which shackles millions of people to great, powerful industries is something foreign to him and something to which he cannot adjust himself. He has never known what it is to be pushed, shoved and ordered about like the clever town-dweller who comes and gapes at him with a sympathetic curiosity.

Preface

Barge-like hulls are the most ancient of all English sailing craft and the art of handling shallow draft vessels has been handed down through hundreds and hundreds of years. It is not a thing you can learn at a university. That the epidemic of mechanisation which has spread all over the world and eliminated the square-rigged sailing ships, schooners and sailing smacks should in time leave the barges rotting in their salty creeks has for long been inevitable. But at least it can be said that when all other wind-driven vessels had gone into history the fleets of spritsail-rigged sailing barges held their own for many years against an ever increasing number of steam and motor ships, and might still have prospered had new hulls been built and new blood encouraged to learn the ways of the sea in the best, though hardest, school.

BOB ROBERTS

Pin Mill
Suffolk

ACKNOWLEDGEMENTS

For permission to use photographs the author wishes to thank Mr Bob Woods, *Eastern Daily Press*, Mr Fred Johnson, Mr Hervey Benham, and Mr S. Platt.

Adventures in the Barge 'Greenhithe'

ON a cold March day in the year 1941 two roughly clad figures might have been seen trudging along the quay of Great Yarmouth harbour, each labouring under a large kitbag and casting hopeful glances in the direction of the Gallon Can, a popular resort for thirsty seamen, situated on the opposite shore, which was due to open its doors to welcome weary rovers into its warmth and hospitality.

Jerry and I had come by train from London to join a new ship, a coastal sailing barge named the *Greenhithe*. He had been my mate in the last of the boom-rigged barges, the old *Martinet*, and she had become a war casualty off Orfordness the week before. We had been washed ashore out of the lifeboat on Aldeburgh's shingly beach and after a few days' rest had been appointed master and mate of the *Greenhithe*.

The barge was named after a little Thames side village in Kent where her owners, the Everard family, had built up a famous coastwise shipping company out of what had been a quiet old barge yard. There were scores of swift, sleek motor ships in the firm in these days of hurry-scurry, but the late Mr Everard, faithful to the picturesque craft which had laid the foundation of the firm, had insisted at his death that the sailing barges be kept in commission and found permanent employment. This request his sons had duly carried out and as long as crews could be found the sailormen formed a useful little fleet in the company's system of coastal transport. And the hard ways of sail trained many a resourceful seaman for the comparatively easy job of handling ships under power.

Yarmouth harbour is formed by two and a half miles of quays built along the banks of the River Yare. As we walked along we saw little trawlers (all bristling with guns for their war-time duties), big steamships up to three thousand tons, the Navy's motor torpedo boats, small coasters and various craft such as local shrimpers, launches and laid-up yachts. Towering rather snobbishly over this heterogeneous collection of vessels were the lofty spars of the *Greenhithe*, her long bowsprit topped up and her red sails stowed neatly in their brails.

As we came round a bend in the wharf we could see that her hull was mottled with rust, her spars dirty and her rigging unkempt. Looking at her from the quay she presented an abject and forlorn appearance, as all sailing vessels do when left unattended for any length of time.

For several months she had been in this berth, her skipper on a sick bed and her disheartened crew departed.

Her iron decks sounded strange to our feet as we jumped aboard, the resounding 'bong' being very different from the familiar 'thud' on the solid oak of the old *Martinet*. After being in a wooden ship a hull of steel and iron seems a soulless thing, but the saving grace of the *Greenhithe* was a pretty sheer and a head on her as bold as the North Foreland.

She had been built in 1923 in Fellowes yard at Great Yarmouth, where many a trawler and herring drifter had been launched, and the rise of her foredeck was more akin to that of a fishing vessel than a flat-bottomed barge.

She was reported to be cranky in a strong breeze and liable to heel over at an alarming angle. This proved to be true enough and she was certainly not a ship for a man with

2

shaky nerves; but her high ends made her a tough customer in heavy weather and she would ride like a lifeboat to her cables or hove-to under canvas.

Her rig was arranged in the usual manner of spritsail barges except that she sported a mule mizzen — that is, an after mast high enough to carry a sail bent to a boom and gaff.

The mainmast was forty-seven feet high with a forty-two foot topmast above it, the two overlapping ten feet at the mainmast head, making a total height above the deck of seventy-nine feet. Her sprit, which holds out the peak of the mainsail and the topsail sheet, was fifty-nine feet eight inches. The bowsprit was a stout pitch pine spar of thirty-six feet, so when it was topped up the end of it was nearly as high as the hounds.

Her wooden wheelhouse aft, which was normally a whaleback affair open on the foreside, had been boxed in by great concrete slabs and reinforced by a steel roof and doors to protect the helmsman from the missiles of the enemy. Although we were not aware of it at the time, this miniature blockhouse was shortly to play quite a big part in our lives and fortunes.

I had often stepped aboard the *Greenhithe* for a yarn with young George Dray, who had been skipper of her for the past five years, but I had never been below in her cabin. So when we went down the scuttle hatch I was impressed by the vast amount of locker space, the waste of floor space, the number of unnecessary projections and corners, the excellence of the pitch pine panelling, the splendid brass lamp which hung from one of the beams, the inadequacy of the little fireplace, and a proverbial inability to swing a cat round.

There was a skipper's state-room and a mate's state-room, each comprising a bunk and sufficient space to put your feet down before emerging into the cabin proper. The master's state-room was damp and stuffy and the mate's had no access to the warmth of the cabin, being almost directly under the scuttle hatch and actually outside the cabin door. I learned later that no mate of the *Greenhithe* had ever endured more than one night in this state-room (ironical term!) and had always slept in the forecastle, which was well heated, airy and comfortable. In fact, except for the lack of polished panelling, the forecastle was a better place to live in than the captain's quarters aft. But tradition must be respected, and I was doomed to languish in musty dignity while the crew slept in comfort forward.

In the end, Jerry and I decided, after a brief but critical survey of our new ship, that for all her faults and graces, she could be made into a good little vessel to work and live in and a profitable one into the bargain if Dame Fortune would but smile on us occasionally. We therefore dumped our kit-bags and sculled across the river to the beckoning lights of the Gallon Can, there to embrace a couple of pints and drink to the health of our new ship.

We met George Dray during the evening, pale and ill-looking and muffled up to the eyebrows like a steamboat sailor. He had always had bad luck in her and according to him she was 'a cow for bearing up' and 'a poor tool to windward'. While he was in her she had been driven ashore on Yarmouth beach and had more than once lost all her sails.

We spent the next day getting the barge ready for sea and then boldly ordered the tug *George Jewson* to take us out the following morning. There was a fresh north-east wind and every prospect of a quick passage to London. An empty barge will go like the devil before the wind and we were soon to learn that one of the virtues of the *Greenhithe* was that she would march along at a fine rate of knots as long as she had a slack sheet.

It was a strong wind and during the squalls and hard puffs it took two of us to steer her. Her rudder was not deep enough and as we ran southward past Lowestoft and Yarmouth her stern rose to a short, steep following sea and the tail of the rudder was almost out of the water.

It was ten o'clock in the morning when the tug let us go at Yarmouth pierheads and at dusk we anchored off Clacton, having run a distance of sixty-two miles in eight hours.

Being war-time we were compelled to anchor at sunset when in the Thames Estuary or within three miles of the British coast owing to military precautions against the danger of an invasion by the Germans. The *Greenhithe* was armed with a twenty-seven year old Canadian rifle and a thirty year old machine-gun for use against aeroplanes, E boats, armed raiders or, if necessary, to withstand a full scale attack by the German Navy.

This run up from Yarmouth made us think that, with some alteration in her gear and a piece put on the bottom of her rudder, the *Greenhithe* was not such a bad barge as Skipper Dray made her out to be.

Back in London River we had but little time to do much with her rigging or even to scrub the weeds and barnacles off her. She was fixed for a cargo of cement up-river to the West India Dock and also to load rice out of a steamship lying in the same dock. The rice was for Norwich. The owners had therefore given us a flying start with our new ship and for a time we were too busy making money to do much to the barge.

Shortly after this we were engaged in a fairly regular trade of carrying cement from London River to Yarmouth, about 175 tons a time, although we were occasionally diverted into other trades, such as fertiliser for Whitstable, wheat for Lowestoft, linseed for Ipswich, and cement for Colchester. It was while coming back empty from one of these trips to Yarmouth that we became involved in a one-sided battle with the Highland Light Infantry, who were positioned in forts and blockhouses along the beaches and cliffs to the southward of Lowestoft. These bonny Highlanders soon altered our gear for us but not quite as we wanted it altered.

It was a fine, cold bright day and the barge was idling along about a mile from the shore. Jerry, the mate, was supervising a delicious smelling stew which was bubbling merrily on the forecastle stove. As I stood at the wheel, occasionally getting a waft of appetising fumes coming up through the cabin skylight I thought how peaceful the world seemed and how little like the days of a mighty and destructive war which was going on over half the world. The sea was calm and there was hardly enough wind to fill our sails. And that stew did smell good!

'I'll give it another five minutes', Jerry called out, 'the spuds aren't quite done.'

Just at that moment a peculiar noise passed over the barge followed by a sharp crack from the shore. I realised after a moment or two that it was a rifle shot.

It was followed by another, and two small holes appeared in our mainsail.

'Jerry,' I said, 'come up here a minute. There's some silly blighter firing at us.'

The mate stuck his head out of the scuttle and was indulging in some disparaging comments on the riflemen when there was a rat-tat-tat-tat — and a stream of machine-gun bullets swept across our main hatches. It was as well the *Greenhithe* had been given that steel and concrete wheelhouse. In an amazingly short time Jerry and I prostrated ourselves on the deck within this cramped but comforting enclosure.

The machine-gunning continued almost without a break. I made a bold dash from the wheelhouse to the cabin ladder, a distance of fully four feet, (it seemed like four miles to me!) and descended at surprising speed. Below I grabbed hold of our three recognition flags given us by the Naval Control authorities. Jerry made a gallant sortie to the mizzen signal halliards, bent the flags and hoisted them. This action was greeted with a burst of fire of re-doubled intensity and as we scuttled back to our wheelhouse like a couple of rabbits diving into a warren, the flags went fluttering down into the water, the halliards shot clean in half.

We lay for a while wondering what was going to happen to us. Our sail looked like a pepper box and the hatch cloths were ripped into ribbons by the bullets.

Once more I made a jump for the cabin ladder and got hold of a big red ensign. We ran out on deck and hastily tied it in the mizzen rigging. Five minutes later it was no more, shot away like the signal flags.

So we resumed our prostrations and discussed the possibility of the soldiers bringing up some sort of heavy armament to blow us to smithereens. I cursed and swore out of sheer fright but Jerry was as cool as a cucumber and quietly remarked 'I can smell the stew burning.' So it was. My remarks on the British Army in general and the Highland Light Infantry in particular were enough to burn anything.

Presently there was a loud explosion on our foredeck. I saw part of the big cog-wheel of our anchor windlass sailing through the air to hit the starboard shrouds and fall on the mastcase. Jerry, who had once been a soldier for a short time, guessed that they had dropped a mortar shell on us.

All this time the barge had been driving to the southward on the flood tide towards Benacre Point, practically becalmed so that there was no hope of getting out of range of these over-zealous warriors. Equally tantalising was the fact that out on the horizon we could see naval patrol boats and minesweepers and not far away the harbour and town of Lowestoft. I thought that war or no war, it would be hard luck to be killed in such a situation by one's own countrymen.

It seemed an age that we lay on our stomachs in that wheelhouse. We could see that many of our ropes and wires had had a strand shot through and the rails and hatches looked a shambles. At last we drifted past the last of the line of forts and gradually the firing died away with a few stray bursts.

We breathed a sigh of relief. The decks were in an awful mess but we were still afloat. And we were still alive. The stew was burnt to a hopeless evil smelling mess. As we set about knotting and splicing the rigging a little breeze came from the north and carried us round Orfordness so that we could anchor for the night in Hollesley Bay. No vessel came to our assistance, no signal was made to us from the shore. Indignant and obstinate, we refrained from asking for help, reserving our pent up rage to concentrate on a vigorous complaint to the proper quarter.

Next day there was a beautiful easterly breeze and having wedged up the remains of the windlass so that we could heave up our anchor we sailed up to Greenhithe and laid the facts before Mr William Everard, one of the three brothers who owned and managed the company. He took the matter up with the War Office and eventually let them off lightly by making them pay just for the damage they had done.

So far as Jerry and I were concerned it meant a week on the yard for repairs and at last we were able to re-adjust the rigging and sails more to our liking. We hove the mainmast and topmast farther forward, set up the main rigging and slacked the collar lashing about two inches. We did not have time to do any more as we were required to load cement for Yarmouth over at Gray's. Our alterations may seem rather infinitesimal but they made a lot of difference to the set of the sails.

Freak Storm

TRADING between London and Yarmouth in a sailing barge gives the crew enough thrills, enough excitement and a rough life generally without the added anxieties of making passages in times of war. There is the unending battle of wits with the winds and tides, using the elements, whether boisterous or gentle, to serve the ship and take her to her destination while always facing the possibility that they might frustrate, obstruct, or even destroy her. In a barge like the *Greenhithe* we have only eleven inches of freeboard (the amount of the ship's side out of the water) when loaded, and that is not very much when running a beam swell in the North Sea. So the skipper has to employ a judgement which comes of long experience and employ a sea-sense which must combine the elements of a steady nerve, a confidence in his own decisions and the courage to put them into effect.

Jerry and I found that the war made us work harder and take risks which we would not otherwise have done, in addition to facing the customary onslaughts of the enemy. So when I tell you that one day we nearly lost our barge and our own lives as well through taking a chance with the weather, the reader will appreciate that such risks had to be taken throughout the years of war in order to make our passages, deliver our cargoes and at the same time earn a reasonable living.

We were loaded with 180 tons of cement and had run down through the estuary from London River with a smart westerly breeze on our quarter. By the time we were off Harwich the weather began to look threatening and there was only an hour's daylight to spend. The sky was smooth and grey and the outline of the land stood out stark and clear in the gathering gloom. In normal times we would have sought the protection of an anchorage in the Rolling Grounds so that in the case of very bad weather coming upon us we could slip into Harwich harbour.

But this was war-time. We must not be under way after dark under penalty of being fired on by our own aircraft, warships and coast defence batteries. There was a boom across Harwich harbour with a narrow gateway which was shut at nights and did not open again (not for a barge anyway) until after daybreak. Moreover, to go into Harwich harbour was to endure the inevitable delays entailed by having to go ashore and get fresh instructions from the Naval Control, whose officers did not always seem to appreciate the essentials of going to sea under sail.

We always disobeyed the routing instructions and warnings handed out to us by the Naval Control, although it was pleasant to call at their various offices when we had time to spare and chat over a cup of tea with the young ladies of the Women's Royal Naval Service, which seemed to have collared all the best looking girls in England.

So on this particular night we kept away from the temptations of a quiet night in Harwich, told the examination boat at the Cork that we were bound to Bawdsey (I blush to think of the lies I used to shout to those chaps for fear they would order me into harbour and spoil a good passage) and ran down inside the Cutler to Hollesley Bay, where we anchored, just abreast of Orford Haven. There were no Naval Control boats as far down as this so we reckoned that we had shaken them off and were free to make our way to Yarmouth in the morning.

The old *Greenhithe* rolled and wallowed as she laid athwart the weather-going flood tide but our anchor was in good holding ground and Jerry and I, after a hot meal, settled down to a game of chess. We often played chess if we were brought up for the night in an exposed anchorage as we got rather tired of reading and listening to the everlasting dance bands on the wireless. Although Jerry used to win about three games to my one, we were fairly evenly matched and the night hours rolled by with amazing rapidity.

About midnight, after a look round on deck to see that everything was well stowed and the barge riding safely, we turned in, setting the alarm for five o'clock so that we would have time for a cup of tea before mustering at dawn.

When we got under way the next day there was a moderate westerly breeze, and although the sunrise was a glowering red I had hopes that within a few hours we would sail the thirty odd miles to Yarmouth in smooth water with an off-shore wind on our quarter.

Under all plain sail and the bowsprit jib, we headed north past the snug little town of Aldeburgh and the sand dunes of Thorpeness, until we were almost abreast of Southwold. The town of Southwold, with a lighthouse in the middle of it, stands on fairly high ground and its houses and streets are always plain from the sea. But on this particular morning the visibility was phenomenal and although the barge was about half a mile off shore we could distinguish the knockers on the doors, a man without a hat leading a little black dog, a woman cleaning windows, a cat crossing a green — just as if we were standing in the town itself. I thought I saw a fly crawling up the lighthouse, but I couldn't swear to it.

Then the sky seemed to be pervaded by a peculiar light and a great arc of white spread upwards from behind the town. It was just like the glare from some giant lamp and the stark look which it gave to the outline of the shore and the rooftops seemed nothing short of wicked.

'What do you reckon it is? A squall?' said Jerry, drawing off his umpteenth cup of tea.

'It's a squall all right,' I answered. 'Drop the head of our topsail down and pick up a bit on your main brails.'

Down came the topsail with a rattle and a few clinks on the winch drew up two cloths of the mainsail as I eased away the sheet. Feeling that we were now ready for whatever was in store for us Jerry came aft and stood by the wheelhouse.

As we expected, the wind came upon us with a sudden violence. Over went the *Greenhithe* like a boxer swaying away from a punch. She was never stiff in a breeze and always inclined to sprawl over in heavy weather, so on this occasion it was only a matter of seconds before her lee rail, from the fore-horse to the main-horse disappeared under a welter of bubble and foam. Jerry sprang to lee side of the wheel and together we got the helm up so that the barge could run off the wind and thus ease the pressure on her canvas. In an ordinary gale or heavy squall we would have been quite safe, apart from being forced off our proper course, but this seemed to be half a dozen squalls wrapped up in one. Gradually, against her helm, the barge began to creep up into the wind again as it blew harder.

'Ease that mainsheet and pick up as much of the mainsail as you can — all of it if you can — keep the block hooked.'

The mate was quick, strong and courageous. For some unknown reason I have always been blessed with good mates and Jerry was the best of them all. Bit by bit he reduced the bellying red sail, first on the main brail, which is of wire, and then on the middle and lower brails, which are of two inch rope and go round the sail in the form of a long bow-line. Every now and then he splashed his way aft to ease off a bit more of the mainsheet, until at last the sail was tightly stowed up, peak brails and all, and we were scudding before the onslaught under foresail and topsail sheet. I could not leave the wheel to help him for fear the barge would broach-to or gybe.

To stow up a barge's mainsail may not seem a very big job to people who have seen it done smartly in a river or sheltered creek: but in a big coasting barge, with a blast fierce enough to blow a strong man overboard, it is a different matter. Enveloped in spray and the water swirling round him knee deep, I felt thankful for his strength and determination.

There was not a hope of holding the barge under the land and by the time Jerry had got the sail off her we were two or three miles from the shore. The wind was west, screeching through the rigging like a horde of devils, and the best we could do was to run east-north-east with the wind on the port quarter.

Our 180 tons of cement did not exactly help us so far as buoyancy was concerned and very soon heavy seas began thumping down across the main-horse and I began to worry about the wedges. If one or two of them were to come out and the wind and water lift the tarpaulins, the seas would take off the hatches, break down into the hold and quickly put an end to both the *Greenhithe* and her crew.

What at first seemed to be a fierce squall now resolved itself into a violent gale. I kept saying to Jerry, 'it can't keep on blowing as hard as this.' But it did.

Within an hour there were steep breaking seas sweeping across the barge and I think we were both privately praying that the foresail sheet would stand the strain; for if we lost our foresail we should lose control of the vessel and no longer be able to keep her stern on to the weather. And in that case we should be extremely fortunate to survive.

We dare not let that foresail even quiver. We knew that our lives depended on it. Had the wind flown into the north-west we would have chanced gybing her to get back under the lee of the land.

We saw a small motor ship through the white haze of flying spray, staggering to windward with the seas breaking clean across her forecastle head. It was only a fleeting

13

glimpse but she looked to be in as bad a pickle as we were but as far as I could make out her skipper was tacking her to windward like a sailing ship. It flashed through my mind at the time that whoever was handling her was no steam-boatman, and we learned some days later that it was Jimmy Mole in the Signality. He had spent his life in sailing barges and had been master of the 285 tons *Alf Everard* before he went into power craft.

Fine seaman though he is, he could not do anything to help us and his crew thought that we were almost certainly doomed to destruction. He told me afterwards that he had to tack his ship all the way through Yarmouth Roads 'just as if she were a barge.' When he finally got into harbour he immediately phoned Mr William Everard in London and told him of his fears for the *Greenhithe*. At once, every possible form of assistance was set in motion. Ships were warned to keep a look out for us, coastguards were informed, lifeboats ordered out to search and even the R.A.F. was notified.

Little could any of them have done except stand by us in case the barge foundered for in such a sea no one could have taken us off and to have jumped in the water would have been suicide.

Unaware of all these powers summoned to assist us, we charged wildly across the North Sea in the general direction of Germany. Desperately we clung to the wheel, pulling and heaving this way and that in order to keep her end on to the seas. We were pooped again and again and the decks and hatches were continually a welter of swirling, breaking water. It would have been impossible for a man to make his way forward of the main-horse without facing the certainty of being washed overboard: and even to traverse the quarter decks but a few feet from the wheelhouse would have been a risky venture.

But we dare not budge from our stance at the wheel lest she broach-to or gybe the foresail to destruction.

Once a great wave crashed right over the top of the wheel-house so that for several moments we could not see what was happening. Then as the water careered forward, Jerry jerked his head in the direction of the boat davits. I glanced across. The boat had gone and on the fore davit, which was bent drunkenly downwards, swung the splintered stem post, as if wrenched out of the boat by some enraged giant. On the after davit there dangled only the ring bolt of the stern post. That was all that remained of our lifeboat.

Shortly afterwards we shipped another such sea, and as the towering wall of water engulfed the after decks a great banging and cracking was set up like a display of fireworks. Our lifebelts in the mizzen rigging had been carried away and the acetelyne flares attached to them had been torn off. With a sizzling noise and a series of loud reports they jumped round the decks as the barge reared up and shook the water from her, and then they disappeared over the side.

I was anxious and a bit afraid. This was the most desperate situation I had ever had to face in all my years at sea. Even at the time of writing, years after, I still regard it as the time when hope and courage had sunk to the feeblest flicker. I had once been caught in the tail-end of a West Indian hurricane in a twenty-seven foot boat; I had faced starvation and thirst in the tropical doldrums; I had drifted for weeks in a dismasted derelict in the Pacific; I had (like many others) experienced some bad moments from bombs and bullets in the stress of war; — but this was the blackest day of all.

I looked across at Jerry. His unshaven face was caked white with salt and he looked set and serious. He, too, was wondering what our chances were.

'What do you think of things?' he shouted. He had to shout although he was only a few feet away.

I had already sorted out the possibilities of our immediate future and being somewhat breathless and tired I had to sum them up as briefly as possible.

'If the barge doesn't sink, and we don't blow up on the mine barrier, we can keep running like this until we get to the other side — should fetch somewhere between Terschelling and Heligoland. Then, if we don't blow up on the German mine barrier, or get shot to hell, or get sunk by an aeroplane, the best we can hope for is to put her ashore and get taken prisoner. I suppose their beaches are mined the same as ours but we'll have to chance that. Of course, if the wind flies into the north-west we'll chance that foresail with a gybe and we'll have a good chance of getting back to dear old England. I reckon this wind 'll norther out in time — must do, surely. Can't blow like this much longer without flying. One thing — there won't be many German bombers about this weather'.

Jerry looked very solemn for a while. Like me, he was a married man with a family. Then he laughed as if it was no good worrying anyway.

'If all goes well, shall we be Oflag or Stalag?'

'Captain and chief officer — Oflag I should think.'

Jerry lapsed into silence for a little while. He had another alternative in mind.

'What about English spies? Washed up. No uniforms. No papers.' He drew his finger across his throat. That was another possibility.

There were no squalls, no rain, no lulls. Overhead the whitish grey clouds hustled across the sky and the haze of driving spray linked one wave with another.

On and on we went, wondering what the end would be. Our brief bits of conversation petered out. We became too tired, too thirsty (perhaps too anxious) to talk. We had no idea of the passage of time but I guessed by the light that the sun was well past its zenith when I noticed some small buoys with flags on them. I pointed them out to Jerry. He nodded and knew what I meant. It was the mine barrier, laid up through the North Sea to give protection to British coastal shipping from attacks by the larger vessels of the German Navy.

All I knew about mine barriers was gleaned from hearsay, but I had been told that they were moored about nine feet below the surface. I did not know whether this nine feet referred to low water, but, as it happened, by the time we got to it it must have been just about high water. We were drawing seven feet six inches. I prayed that the drop in the troughs would be cancelled by the height of the tide because it seemed that it would be a cruel stroke of fate to win a battle against the fury of the elements only to be destroyed by some wicked device of mankind.

Nothing happened. The *Greenhithe* continued to pitch her way to the eastward and soon the little flags were lost to sight. We saw no more and I hoped that we were clear.

I was just making a rough calculation that we were about thirty miles off the Norfolk coast when the great moment came. We both noticed it at the same time. I pointed to the compass and Jerry nodded. The grime and brine on his face cracked into a smile.

We were still before the wind but steering *east-south-east* instead of east-north-east as hitherto. The wind had northered.

For a while we plunged on along the new course while I conjured up a mental map of the North Sea and where we were now likely to arrive. I decided that the time had come to gybe the foresail. Jerry agreed that with the shift of wind it was now or never.

With our hearts aflutter we bore up on the helm. For one awful moment the foresail lifted as if to flog and then — whang — the chain sheet flew across the iron horse with a stream of sparks, fetched up with a quiver on the port side — and held. The sail bellied out once more and all was well. We had gybed at last.

With the wind on the starboard quarter we now headed south-south-east. That meant at least that our fate was put off for a time for on such a course we would not arrive in Holland or Belgium until morning and the weather would have time to moderate. The barge was still being swept by heavy seas, and occasionally pooped into the bargain, but the foresail was still whole and doing its job manfully.

By this time the tide was ebbing away to the northward and I knew that if only the wind would come right northerly we could bring the barge's head to the west of south and then have the tide on our lee bow, helping to check her back towards the English shore.

Whether my traditional good luck refused to leave me or whether the Lord of Storms decided to forget my sins of the past I do not know — but the very shift of wind we wanted came to pass. Towards evening we were heading south-west, and, although still blowing a gale, the seas did not crash down quite so frequently on the main hatches. We were so pleased that we forgot all about the mine barrier and must have crossed back over it again.

Before daylight failed we caught a glimpse of the land and as we came close to it we made out the wooded hills which overlook Aldeburgh. Soon we saw a big white boat tumbling through the breaking seas. It was the Aldeburgh lifeboat, which had been searching for us, and she came near enough to hail and learn that all was well. Although we did not now need their assistance it afforded me no small measure of encouragement to see those stalwart figures in their yellow oilskins and south westers, every one of them a picture of the traditional British seaman.

'We'll run for Harwich,' I shouted, and they waved us farewell and headed for the shore, glad, no doubt, to end their search once they knew that we were safe.

There was still enough wind to give us a speed of about five knots with only the foresail set; but once we had negotiated the turbulent tide rip off Orfordness and gained the smoother water of Hollesley Bay, Jerry was able to leave the wheel and slack the main brail sufficiently to luff us under the lee of the land.

That night we anchored off Bawdsey. I was still unwilling to place the *Greenhithe* within the aegis of the Harwich Naval Control regulations, so rather than go into the comfort of the harbour we laid out in the open with the protection of a friendly weather shore.

Weary and hungry, blood eyed and stiff, we gave her thirty-five fathoms of chain in four fathoms of water, put a tight stow on the mainsail and foresail, and tumbled below.

The cabin was a shambles. Everything was wet and dripping but such minor discomforts were discounted in our desire to get the fire alight and cook some food. The frying pan sizzled, tins were ripped open, the remains of a leg of lamb disappeared as if by magic. To the best of my recollection we demolished a week's rations at one fell swoop. Then we laid down for five hours of glorious slumber.

The sun was up when I awoke. Stiff and sore, I creaked into action and went on deck. The wind had died right away, the sea was smooth and a fine weather haze hung over the land. I called Jerry and we fell to with hot coffee and beans on toast (alas! the old bacon and eggs had become a thing of the past). Thus reinforced, we cleared up the tangle of gear on deck and stowed up the remnants of the topsail, which decorated our rigging and cross-trees like so many gala streamers.

While we were thus engaged a pleasant little breeze began to flutter our flag and, behold! — it was from the west-south-west, the best wind you can have for a run to Yarmouth. We hove in that thirty-five fathoms of chain, set the staysail upside down in place of the topsail, squared away the mainsail — and so to Yarmouth before night fell.

In the morning the manager of the wharf came to see me about discharging the cargo. He seemed rather annoyed. 'We heard that you were on the way and we were expecting you to be here yesterday,' he grumbled. 'I don't know whether I can get enough labour today.'

19

I said I was very sorry but that the weather had not been very good. He seemed to think this was just an excuse for wasting time and went on his way dissatisfied. Eventually, enough dock labourers were found but I had to pay them extra 'beer money' to get the barge empty by the week-end.

'Beer money' has always been a matter of contention between dockers and barge skippers. In the old days the dockers used to leave a clean hold after discharging, or when loading go to extra trouble to stow a cargo so that the vessel could carry her maximum weight. For this they were generally rewarded by a shilling or two from the skipper's pocket. But in more modern times this 'beer money' business became more of a bribe to do the job reasonably well rather than a reward for extra trouble. The dockers sometimes demand 'beer money' even when the work they have done is very far from satisfactory from the bargeman's point of view. It becomes a matter of 'pay up, or we'll do the job badly'. This generally happens in the big ports.

The best answer I have ever heard to such a demand was from seventy-two year old George Cowell when he was master of the *Lady Marjorie*. She was unloading cement into a big ship in the Royal Albert Dock in London and it was close on Saturday midday. George had been walking the deck, muttering about the slowness of the dockers and the all-too-frequent stoppages for cups of tea and arguments, hoping against hope that they would be done in time for him to get back down the river and be home for Sunday dinner.

Now and then he would urge them to get on with the job and at last the final 'board' went up out of the hatchway. Immediately George and his seventy-four year old brother Bill, who was mate, set about getting the beams and hatches on and clearing up to be ready for undocking. While they were busy one of the dockers clambered back aboard and said:

CAMBRIA, *last of the old sailing coasters, with* 5,000 *square feet of canvas set and a crew of two.*

Fine weather and an easy run.

People still come out on the pier to see a barge come in under sail. The GREENHITHE *entering Yarmouth Haven.*

Bargeman's blessing—a fair wind.

The author (left) with Paddy O'Donnell—third hand, mate, and eventually master of the WILL EVERARD.

Barge GREENHITHE *in the Humber coal trade.*

CAMBRIA *loaded and ready for sea.*

Bill Evans, mate of the CAMBRIA.

Race day.

DREADNOUGHT—*for racing.*

CAMBRIA—*for work.*

Light airs.

Lofty spars in a handsome barge. CAMBRIA *does not look like a collier, but she has just unloaded coal.*

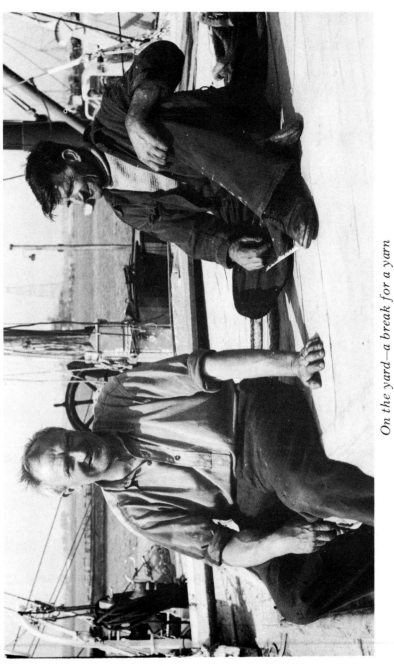

On the yard—a break for a yarn

Big as she was the CAMBRIA *was pretty handy—here she is rushing up in narrow waters past Maldon Town quay to make the High Water on to Green's mill.*

We didn't see our lee rail for three tides

Stacky barges bound up River

My old sailing smack STORMY PETREL

'What about the "beer money" skipper. We got you out just in time or you'd have been here till Monday.'

George straightened his back, pushed back his cheese-cutter hat and scratched his white hair.

'Beer money?' he said, 'Oh, yes. You got change for a quid?'

'Yes, I can change a quid,' replied the docker eagerly, anticipating a handsome tip.

'Well then,' said George briefly, bending to pick up another hatch, 'you don't *need* any "beer money".'

Sunk in the Thames

———————— ❖ ————————

ON the night that the Germans started to bombard England
with flying bombs my barge was waiting to load cement
for Colchester at the Kent Works in Long Reach. I went
home to Bexley to enjoy a few hours of normal civilised
existence but soon discovered that my house was an exceed-
ingly dangerous spot to be in, much more dangerous than
being aboard a barge in London River.

As those devilish contraptions came roaring and hurtling
over the housetops and crashing among the streets of the
suburban towns and villages with terrifying explosions, my
wife and baby crouched under a steel table which served as
a shelter, trying to snatch a few hours sleep. But there was
little or no sleep to be had that night, or in the days and
nights that followed.

I could not go away to sea and leave them to this so my
wife packed a couple of suitcases and brought the babe
aboard the *Greenhithe*. It was safer there. There were no
buildings to fall on them, no flying glass and mortal splinters.
Only a direct hit or a very near miss would bring disaster.

We finished loading on Saturday and on Sunday morning
we got under way. It was a beautiful, warm June day. With
mainsail, topsail, foresail, mizzen and staysail we tacked
slowly down St Clements Reach with a light breeze from
the north-east, working the eddy down along the Kentish

shore while the last of the flood spent itself on the other side of the river.

Soon we had a hail from the *Sara*, the famous racing champion, running up under her huge spread of canvas with the portly Phil Finch at the wheel and his mate Bill setting a big staysail to try and save the high water at Greenhithe. She looked splendid in those days, with her grey sides fresh and clean and the gilt scrolls shining in the sunlight. Phil was a Mistley man, one of a famous barge racing family, and he was very particular about the appearance of his barge. Bill, who had been mate of her for over ten years, also took a pride in keeping her in spotless condition.

They saw my little daughter's golden head bobbing round the wheelhouse and the missus sitting on the cabin skylight and waved us all a cheerful farewell. Close astern of them came old Knocker, sailing the *Leonard Piper*, and he too called out and wished us a good passage.

Little did they know — or we — what tragedy was in store for us that day.

We had just rounded the Ovens buoy at the eastern end of Gravesend Reach and entered the Lower Hope when I noticed a big steamship coming astern of us; but as by then we were clear of most of the power traffic I was not unduly worried about a single vessel in such a broad reach as this.

Although past high water the tide was still eddying up-river on the Essex side so I put the barge about in midstream and tacked to the southward. The big steamship was round the Ovens by then and shaping down the Hope, but I could see all her starboard side so assumed that she would pass under our stern.

Anne was playing down in the cabin and Ginger was tending the foresail bowline while Jerry saw to the staysail sheets. Jerry came aft and stood on the quarter deck and then I saw a look of alarm come over his face.

'Bob, she's coming the wrong side of us. She's starboard helm.' I dodged out of the wheelhouse for a moment (one could not get a very good view from inside owing to it being bricked up as a war-time shelter) and saw to my dismay her great bow bearing down on us. I thought that she would blow port (two blasts) or starboard (one blast), as is usual in the river, to give us some idea of what she was going to do. But no sound came from her. It was too late to wind again and in any case owing to the light weather we had not enough way to come round quickly.

On she came, like a great juggernaut bent on our destruction. Her mighty bow towered over us. With a sickening jolt she struck us amidships on our starboard side, her massive stem ploughing a couple of feet or more into our deck and heeling the barge right over.

At the moment of impact the third hand, like a true Ginger, made one flying leap for the cabin hatch, dropped down and emerged in a second with the babe in his arms.

Jerry and I dashed to the lifeboat davits, feverishly cast off the lashings and dropped the boat into the water. It was fortunate, being on the starboard side, that it had not been crushed by the ship but the *Greenhithe* hung at right angles to her stem and she kept coming slowly ahead to keep the hole filled while we got away in the boat. I got the wife and babe into the boat with Jerry in charge. He was a clear-headed, capable seaman and knew what to do.

Then the ship went astern, drawing her stem out of the hole, and the water rushed into the vitals of the barge. But as she heeled her sails filled and she began to gather way. Instead of jumping into the lifeboat I sprang to the wheel and pulled the helm hard up.

'Take care of them,' I shouted to Jerry, 'I'm going to try and beach her.' Seeing what I intended young Ginger scrambled back aboard to help me, but it was a forlorn hope.

A small Naval tug named the *Dido* came steaming up but the barge went over and over until I could see that she was going to sink. I picked up a pair of lifejackets and handed one to Ginger. We stood on the port quarter as it rose up in the air and her bottom showed above the water.

'Jump, Ginger, jump.'

Onlookers said they saw two splashes and I remember getting a mouthful of River Thames, which is salt water enriched by mud, sewage, chemicals and whatnot. The *Dido* steamed up and half a dozen lifebuoys came flying through the air.

They got Ginger aboard first. When I came to the surface I saw Jerry keeping the lifeboat clear and my wife (somewhat scared and stunned by these sudden happenings) sitting on the middle thwart with the baby clutched in her arms. About twenty yards away was the *Greenhithe*. I could see her bottom coming up as she went over. Backing clear was the monster who had destroyed her.

As the barge rolled on to her side in her final agony, with the masts and sails in the water, there came a loud explosion and a column of water shot up as the air in her hold burst open the hatches. The underwater concussion sent me swirling down again and I lost the lifebuoy that the crew of the *Dido* had thrown to me. I frogged to the surface once more, not feeling very happy this time, but the tug skipper was an old Thames waterman and he was soon alongside me and strong young arms reached down and dragged me up on deck, a choking, dripping specimen of a bargeman without a barge.

Then they took Jerry and our somewhat bewildered passengers (who had come aboard the barge because it was too dangerous to stay at home!) out of the lifeboat and we were taken to Cliffe Jetty.

The officer commanding the Naval post there had his men rout out some old clothes and ordered the tug to take us back to Greenhithe. Mr William Everard, who had been informed of the collision, and had ordered a car to take us home, the shipwright foreman and a couple of yard hands were waiting on the causeway like a welcoming committee to a bunch of shipwrecked mariners. As the *Dido* could not get alongside the causeway she transferred us to a small Naval launch, which was in charge of a young rating who seemed anxious to show his ability to run alongside at full speed and then go astern on his engine and stop dead in the old Navy style. Unfortunately he forgot that the ebb stream fell slack close inshore and the launch went head first at the causeway just as we were ready to get ashore. All the welcoming committee saw of us for a moment were our backsides and the soles of our feet.

Blushing and confused, the young coxswain backed astern and tried again. This time we held on tight and managed to keep our feet while Ginger threw the painter ashore and the yard chaps hauled us alongside. But no one had been able to repress a guffaw at the sight of us bottoms up in the boat and this thin streak of humour at least relieved for us the blackness of the day.

We arrived at the house in a dignified style, for it was a very grand car we were in, but this dignity was soon to be lowered by the task of walking up the gravel path in bare feet. Jerry and I were arrayed in bell-bottoms and jerseys but footwear had been unobtainable.

Jerry lived in Wimbledon, the other side of London, but we had a deuce of a job to find him something to put on his feet. Eventually a neighbour discovered a pair of size-ten dancing pumps. So the worthy Jerry, arrayed in an ill-fitting loud check jacket over Naval jersey and slacks, went on his way home looking like something out of a comic opera.

It was Sunday afternoon that we had been sunk. On Monday salvage vessels of the Port of London Authority went to the Lower Hope. A diver went down to inspect the wreck and pass slings under her. On Tuesday's tide the barge was raised clear of the bottom and deposited in shallow water on the Ovens Spit. On Wednesday she was picked up again, carried up river suspended between the salvage lighters, and placed on Everard's yard at Greenhithe.

Rarely have I seen a difficult job done in such a workmanlike and efficient manner in so short a time.

I joined the salvage unit on the Wednesday and came up river with the body of my old ship, rather like the chief mourner at a funeral. The final manoeuvre of putting her on Everard's yard was a masterpiece. The three great lighters were edged between the moorings and the numerous off-lying craft until the wreck was inside everything. A bit more backing and filling, the slings were let go, the lighters extricated and the *Greenhithe* left sitting on the bottom.

When the tide ebbed away the barge was found to be sitting on the built up chalk berth just as perfectly as if she had been put there when afloat under favourable conditions.

Wreck Comes to Life

IF you had walked into Everard's yard at Greenhithe in the middle of June 1944 you would have seen the hulk of a barge lying there, a battered, grimy object with her rigging a tangled heap of ropes and wires strewn across her decks and hatchways.

The mainmast, broken off at the hounds, lay half athwart the deck and the iron mastcase in which the heel normally rested was wrenched into a crazy and almost unrecognisable shape. The sprit, in two pieces, lay across it with the joggle end protruding over the side. Trailing over the side in the mud were the sodden remains of the mainsail, tangled up with some more ropes and wires.

The bowsprit was intact, although a bedraggled grey jib hung forlornly from the end of it like the stricken banner of some defeated knight, the muddy tide having besmirched it with the contents of London River. The mizzen mast had disappeared altogether. So had the wheelhouse. The wheel stood naked and broken, a shattered monument to what had been a live and handsome vessel.

On the starboard side of this pitiful shape was an ugly, perpendicular gash some four feet long, biting into the deck almost as far as the coamings. Fore and aft, the decks were buckled and round her quarters and under the fore rigging were the marks of the salvage vessels lifting wires. All the hatches and beams were gone and the open hold displayed a lopsided heap of solidified cement.

This hulk, this slime covered corpse of a ship, had been the sailing barge *Greenhithe*. Three days ago I had stood to her helm in the blazing sunshine watching her canvas drawing to a cool north-easterly breeze, her movements being those of the thing of life and beauty. Now she lay there looking mishapen and horrible, like a dog that had been run over.

The foreman shipwright walked round her with me and shook his head mournfully. When I dared to mention the word 'repairs' he shrugged his shoulders and mumbled something about 'total loss', as though he was half afraid to tell me that he thought she was done for.

As the water drained out of her I went aboard and clambered gingerly down the cabin hatch, seeking a foothold here and there among the slime, and dropping the last few feet with a squelch on to the mud covered floor.

I can hardly describe what the cabin looked like. Mud, thick and slimy, covered everything — doors, lockers, bunks and panelling. Mattresses, bedding, food, lamps and all the domestic equipment of the cabin was pitched into a revolting and stinking heap, the various articles disguised in a sea of mud and hardly distinguishable one from another. Over in one corner a leg of pork gave off a particularly pungent smell as if to put a final touch of nausea to the scene.

I slithered across to what had been my state-room and thrust my hands into the mud beneath the little row of clothes hooks on the bulkhead. After a while I drew out a disgusting piece of material which I guessed had been my shore-going jacket. It was. In the inside pocket was my wallet. In the wallet were twenty pound notes, sodden but clean.

I took them home and, being a sunny day, nailed them up round the front room window to dry. Passers-by thought that I had either gone crazy or else come into a fortune and papered the drawing room with them. But I was pleased that I had at least recovered something from the wreck. I had been afraid that someone might have 'salvaged' them before I had the chance.

The next day I was off early to the city to see the owners. The two 'guv'nors', Mr Fred and Mr Will, had me into their room and I asked what was to be done with the *Greenhithe* — and with her skipper. Mr Will suggested that I went into one of the motor ships. They were then in process of amassing what was to be the greatest fleet of coasters in the United Kingdom. My heart sank. What the shipwright foreman had said about total loss must have been true. Such faint hopes as I had that the barge would be repaired and re-commissioned faded away.

I thought it was good of them to offer me a start in a power ship, but power ships were not in my line. I had been in sail all my life and had developed a strong prejudice against even the most modern motor and steam vessels, amounting to something akin to contempt.

I thanked them and said that I was not interested in power craft and that if they were not going to repair the *Greenhithe* I would look for a barge elsewhere.

To my surprise Mr Will laughed. He seemed quite relieved to find someone who preferred sailing barges to the easier life in the power craft. He was at heart a lover of barges and on the few evenings when he had nothing to do he would sit in the watchman's hut at the yard, playing crib with the old barge skippers, interrupting the games now and then to enter into argument about chimes and keelsons, leeboards and spars, sailing matches and passage making.

One tale about Mr Will was of a time when he served on the local council. At the meetings each member was provided with a large pad on which to make notes. Mr Will, a hard headed business man, accustomed to making quick decisions, was possibly a little irked at the wordiness of some of the proceedings. One evening, when the meeting had concluded and the councillors were on their way home, someone happened to look at the pad that had been opposite Mr Will's chair. There were not any notes on it about rates, drainage, footpaths, committee reports and such weighty matters. It was covered with diagrams and drawings of sailing barges — stern frames, half sections, different shapes of leeboards, sail plans — nothing about council business!

So you can tell that he was quite pleased to have someone anxious to remain in sailing barges in these days of mechanical progress. He looked across at his brother and said:

'Fred, can we buy a barge for this young fellow; or can you repair the *Greenhithe?*'

Mr Fred was in charge of all repair work and had been foreman of the yard in the days when his father was head of the firm. He was a man of few words but he had an unequalled knowledge of a barge's construction. He carried in his head the measurements of every bolt, beam and trenail of the firm's barges, several of which he had had a hand in building. Moreover, he could make a rapid mental estimate of labour, materials and costs without going into a lot of figures and details.

He leaned back in his chair for a few moments, long enough for me to realise that he was about to pass judgement upon the sorry hulk that lay down on the yard. Would he condemn her? Was she worth spending money on?

'We could repair her in six weeks if we had the hands.'

There and then the whole thing was decided. The barge was to be repaired and re-fitted. The six weeks were likely to stretch into at least as many months owing to so many of the shipwrights being required on the vessels damaged by mines and bombs. It meant that I should have very little help and would have to do much of the labouring work myself as well as rig out.

Back at Greenhithe I met the mate and young Ginger. They had been trying, rather unsuccessfully, to extract their

ruined belongings from the forecastle and had given it up
as a bad job. I explained to Jerry that the repairs to the
barge were likely to occupy some months and asked him
whether he intended to work aboard her on the yard (where
the pay for barge mates was only £2.15.0 a week). He said
that he did not think he could afford to work for £2.15.0 a
week for an indefinite period and was of the opinion that
he had better seek a berth in another barge. I could not
blame him but was sorry to lose him. He had been a good
seaman, a good mate, and a good friend. What better
shipmate can a man expect?

He fitted out the old *Jane* and sailed in her as master,
trading cement in the river for a while and later engaging
in the usual barge trade to Colchester, Ipswich and the
Medway ports.

The *Jane* was an old vessel but as handy as a top when she
was loaded by the stern. Between long spells at the wheel
and short spells at the pump (or sometimes vice-versa),
Jerry achieved some remarkably good passages, once leaving
a whole fleet of barges weather bound at Harwich and
making Plaistow sugar wharf in three tides against a strong
south-west wind.

Before circumstances compelled him to swallow the
anchor and go ashore for good he had become a capable and
respected bargemaster. The years ashore have done him
little harm, for occasionally he comes for a trip to sea with
us — still the same old Jerry, same old wooden clogs and
fisherman's smock, seat out of his pants, a ready smile and
the heart of a lion. I wish there were more like him.

The worthy Ginger, willing to stay on the yard for the
time being, was promoted to mate and soon we set to work
to try and make the *Greenhithe* look more like a barge and
less like something the dustman left behind.

It was a gruelling job, shovelling the mud off the deck
and clearing away the broken spars, sails and rigging, but
with occasional help from the yard crane we got the decks

clear in just over a week so that the labourers could get into the hold and start discharging the cargo. For this job only two old men could be spared and it took them a month, with crowbars and handspikes, to get out the mass of concrete that had been 150 tons of cement in jute sacks.

I had an unholy job in the cabin owing to lack of room to work. I had to get all the mud, muck and rubbish in a great heap in the middle of the floor and then pass it up in bucketloads through the narrow skylight to Ginger. The forecastle, being more roomy, was not so difficult.

I was a fortnight clearing out aft, and then came the washing and scrubbing with hot soda water. But when at last the cabin and two state-rooms were clean and the fire ablaze once more my heart went up a peg. The master's accommodation had begun to look (and smell) more like a cabin and not so much like the bottom of a cesspit.

While all this work was going on giant rockets (known at the time as 'V2') were being fired from the Continent by the German Army and by chance one of these landed in the piggery in Greenhithe village. Apart from killing a lot of pigs, the principal result of the explosion was that practically all the house and shop windows were reduced to small pieces which littered the footpaths and gutters.

As it happens, the best and cleanest way to scrape down discoloured panelling is to use suitably shaped pieces of broken glass. So every morning I walked along the village High Street and set myself up with scrapers for the day. As they blunted I threw them away and went ashore for a fresh lot. In this way I was able to bring the pitch pine panels of the cabin back to an even better condition than they were before the barge was sunk; and with careful sandpapering and varnishing the living quarters aft assumed once more their traditional appearance of respectability.

After painting out the state-rooms and lockers, laying fresh lino on the floor and making a new table, the place was at last fit to live in. The whole job took me six weeks.

In the meantime young Ginger had been shanghaied to another ship and the cleaning out and re-decoration of the forecastle had been left to a couple of elderly yard hands who were not exactly renowned as fast workers and took eight months to make the place habitable.

Not long after, I too, went off to sea in another ship, taking charge of the 270 tons barge *Will Everard* while her regular skipper was on holiday. She seemed a mighty vessel after sailing the *Greenhithe* but, to my surprise, much easier to handle. In moderate weather she carried but little weight on her helm and it was only very rarely that she buried her lee rail as the old *Greenhithe* was apt to do in anything more than a capful of wind. And when she was faced with a twizzle to windward up a narrow creek, such as the upper reaches of the Orwell, I was amazed at the way she would make a board of no more than three or four times her own length and then come about on to the other tack as easily as a yacht.

There used to be four of these big barges in commission under the Everard flag. They were the biggest spritties ever conceived and, to the best of my knowledge, the only sailing barges to be built to a blue print. They were named the *Alf Everard*, *Ethel Everard*, *Fred Everard* and *Will Everard*, being the names of the three brothers and their sister who inherited the business from their father's barge building yard. The performance of these mammoth barges, as some writers have called them, were certainly a credit to the family genius. All of them made splendid passages, pounding the North Sea and Channel winter and summer, dark and daylight, fair weather and foul; yet still able to do bridge and creek work like the smaller barges.

The *Alf* once came out of Weymouth bound to the Humber to load coal; and exactly forty-seven hours later had her anchor down in Hull Roads, having sailed some 500 miles at an average speed of just over ten and a half knots. Her skipper, Jim Mole (a native of the Essex island of Mersea) had only one comment to make. He shrugged his shoulders and said 'Well of course we made a good passage. We had everything in our favour.'

The *Alf* eventually became a motor ship and was lost after the Second World War. Jim Mole, a tough old bird, was crippled in later years by a terrible fall of forty-two feet down a ship's hold with all the hatches crashing on top of him. No one ever expected to see him afloat again. But, nothing daunted, he refused to let that beat him and came back after two years with irons and strappings on his legs to sail the old *Sara* in the races.

You had to be a hard man then in a coasting barge. There was no room for phoneys and line shooters. Tom Willis, from Greenhithe, was another bargeman of the old school. From boy-cook in the boom rigged *Evelyn* he became master of the 280 tons *Ethel*; and the only time I have ever known him ruffled was when he was forced to leave her on the beach at Dunkirk after the evacuation of the British Expeditionary Force. He was prevented by the Navy from going back to her, getting her off and sailing home.

The *Fred* was turned into a motor ship and her old skipper Jesse Farthing, from Harkstead in Suffolk, continued to command her under power. Long after he retired she was sunk in collision in the Thames Estuary.

The *Will* had a 120 horse-power engine installed and at the time of writing is still trading with her canvas cut down to mainsail, foresail and topsail.

For three months I sailed in the *Will* (her regular skipper having a spell ashore) and then I went back to the yard to get on with the reincarnation of the *Greenhithe*. I sought out Alf Naylor, the sailmaker, and together we drew up a fresh sail plan. I wanted more sail area than she used to have. We sketched and re-sketched, rubbed out and altered, until finally we got the whole spread of canvas to fit in with the spars obtainable, the sailmaker's ideas and my notions of what the barge required to make her a bit handier and faster than she had been.

We gave her a topmast of forty-three feet with a long upper cap to rake it well forward. This is a device often used in rigging the racing barges so that a large topsail is carried without giving the vessel an overbearing hoist.

The topmast being well forward, the extra canvas was actually over the fore-hatches. This also avoided the danger of a big sail giving the barge a lot of weather helm.

The mainmast, which had to be of Oregon pine instead of the usual pitch pine, was made to forty-seven feet with a ten foot masthead (i.e. where the mainmast and the topmast overlap).

There was some difficulty in getting a sprit and finally we had the *Ethel Everard's* old one cut down to sixty-one feet three inches.

The wire standing rigging was made by two young riggers, one a little hunchback and the other a barge skipper's son who had become a rigger-sailmaker after serving several years in his father's barge. They had over fifty wire splices to make and in an incredibly short time (less than a week) all the standing rigging was ready. When I came to rig out I found that every eye was the exact size required and every length correct to an inch, which is no small feat of workmanship in these days of 'slap-dash, anyhow, roll on pay-day.'

The only rigging error was in the length of the forestay, which had been sent away for and arrived ready-made, eighteen inches too long. Rather than endure the delay of sending it back to the works I put a chock on the after side of the mainmast above the hounds and substituted a bottle screw for the stem head blocks. Previously the two three-fold iron blocks were kept shipped ready to lower down the gear at any time. But the overlong forestay did not leave room for them. Fiddling about with this blasted forestay

Spinnaker breeze

caused more work, trouble and expense than all the rest of the rigging put together.

When the time came to put the spars and sails aboard the *Greenhithe* I was faced with the task of rigging her with little or no assistance. The yard hands were working all hours of the day and night on war-damaged motor ships. Young Ginger was away in a tanker running 'E Boat Alley', soon to sail deep-sea and win himself rapid promotion. So for a time I laboured alone, shifting heavy gear with blocks and tackles, taking days and days to do a job which, with a little help, would have taken me only a few hours.

The only other barge on the yard was the famous racer *Princess*, whose skipper, Jack Nunn senior, was pottering about the yard, being in ill-health at the time and not always able to work. One day, when I was struggling to get the forty-three feet of topmast into position with the aid of tackles and crab winches I saw him watching me from the shore. I knew that old Jack could never keep away from a barge that was being rigged out but that he never liked to go aboard anyone else's barge in case he might be thought to be interfering.

There he stood, a fine, tall figure, stroking his white moustache and obviously itching to come aboard. After a while I gave him the opening he wanted. I had got the topmast in the caps and there was a heavier job to do.

'Jack, will you lend me a hand to shift the sprit over?'

Jack's blue eyes twinkled.

'Where do you want it?' he asked, although he knew damn well where I wanted it.

'Just up on the coamings so that I can get the muzzle on.'

'Righto. I know where there's a wooden handspike in the sailshop. Just the item for that job. I'll go and fetch it.'

In a few minutes he was aboard — and for every day afterwards until the sails were bent, gear rove, spars up-ended and rigging set up, old Jack was my only assistant. Really I should have been his assistant but he

Racing leeboard

would never allow himself to take charge of anyone else's
barge.

He was one of the finest bargemen who ever put his hand
to a wheel, and although never a coasting man, he had a vast
knowledge of racing and trading under spritsail rig; yet he
would always ask me how I wanted anything done. A pull
here, a hitch there, just at the right time and place and old
Jack was more help than half a dozen strong labourers.

When he felt in need of a breather he would sit on a
bollard while I was tucking splices or serving gear and soon
he would be off round the Mouse Lightship on a race day
'with the *Veronica* and *Queen* to wind'ard and Alf Horlock
trying to shove me down into the slack tide — and I knew
that if I luffed again I'm goin' to let the *Queen* through: so
I bawls out "lee-O, jump to it" and as the hands run

39

forward to tend the sheets I makes as if I'm pulling the
wheel hard down. But I had old Charlie clap the pawl down
and lock the wheel and she kept full. All the others, being
so close aboard of us, came ashiver before they realised that
we weren't coming round. Then we slack off everything
with a run as I up-helm. She darted ahead and by the time
the others straightened up we in sheets and were just that
far enough ahead to have a clear wind. They never saw
nothin' but our old barge's ass after that'.

Jack did not always tell of the races and cups he had won.
He would tell of the times he had lost when he might have
won, of the mistakes he had made and the lessons he had
learnt. And there was nothing Jack Nunn had to say about
barges that was not worth listening to. They were his life,
and always had been.

Old Jack is dead now. He passed away in his little house
by the river at Greenhithe, leaving Young Jack, master of
the *Veronica* and later in charge of the *Lady Maud*, to carry
on with all the knowledge and skill that a father can pass
on to his son.

Long before the hull repairs were completed we had all
the sails bent and rigging rove ready for sea. When at last
the hands could be spared Mr Fred sent them swarming
aboard the *Greenhithe* and the work went ahead like a house
on fire. Plates were cut and rivetted, the rudder assembled
and shipped, leeboards made, and a new steel wheelhouse
constructed. Chippers and painters appeared by the dozen
and before long the *Greenhithe* blossomed forth like a flower
in the Spring, resplendent in all her new clothes, set off by
her shining black rails, grey hull and red bottom.

No stranger would have guessed that fifteen months
before she had been lying at the bottom of the Lower Hope,
full of mud and slime, with a great hole in her side and her
spars but a pile of broken timber. It had been fifteen months
of gruelling work, the triumph of accomplishment marred by
disappointments and delays. But at last the great day came.

Dark Channels

———⊕———

IT was nearly high water and the tide lapped along the sides of the *Greenhithe* as she lifted off the blocks on which she had been put for a final inspection and a few odd jobs round her bottom.

No longer was I working alone. I had acquired a mate and third hand, I could see in the short time that it took to ship the leeboards and haul off to a mooring buoy in the stream that they were a pair of lively lads and not afraid of work.

Jack Woods, the mate, was a young fellow from Yarmouth, twenty-four years old, with a mop of curly yellow hair that had earned him the nickname of 'Blondie' when he had been mate of the *Oxygen*. He was short and small, but barging had made him strong and wiry. He would often despise the use of ratlines when going aloft. With his feet hitched round a backstay he would be up to the topmast head (eighty feet above the deck) in less time than it took many a mate to climb the ratlines to the cross-trees. And he had one great quality apart from his seamanship; a great sense of humour and a love of fun.

The third hand, Ken Fry, although only sixteen, towered above the mate in breadth as well as height. He had been deck boy in a tug for twelve months but his heart was in the barges. The tug-master, an old bargeman himself, told me that he was a 'good lad: but no use keeping him in the tug when his heart is aboard every sailorman we pass in the river.'

This was not altogether surprising. His grandfather had been skipper of a barge. His father had been skipper of a barge. His uncle had been skipper of a barge. And they had all been good bargemen — hard, strict and efficient. In young Ken's home (which was now at Northfleet, although the family came from Brightlingsea) the talk had always been of barges and they had made him familiar with the worst side as well as the best. Although his father, a Freeman of the River, had wanted to apprentice him and make a tug-man out of him, the family tradition was too strong. Ken became a bargeman. And later in these pages the reader can judge for himself what sort of fist he made of it.

The first orders we got were to load coke for Boulogne. This job was cancelled. Then we were expected to load wheat for Norwich. That was cancelled. Then we were fixed to load margarine at Jergen's wharf across the river and take it up to the Upper Pool. We actually sailed across to Jergens and berthed but that job, also, was cancelled because of a dockers' strike in London.

'Blimey,' said the mate, 'we're getting about, aren't we? Boulogne, Norwich, Tower Bridge — all in three days. Look at the money we're earning. I think I'll do a freight down-Channel before I turn in tonight.'

Although all these prospective cargoes came to nothing it was not long before we were at work in earnest. We were to proceed to Ipswich to load sugar for London.

Away we went with a smart westerly breeze, and I was well pleased at the way she handled with her new gear. During the run down the river and out into the Swin and Wallet channels we did not see a single barge we could try her against but I could tell that she was certainly faster and handier than she had been before she had been put down the cellar.

In Ipswich Dock we loaded 165 tons of raw sugar, straight from the factory, warm, brown and damp. Out of the spillings the mate concocted a large stock of toffee, with the aid of some butter and a dash of vinegar. The flavour was excellent but the texture gave me an uneasy and rather too vivid impression of what it must be like to suffer from lockjaw.

We came out of the dock astern of the *Cambria* and the *Dannebrog*. The *Cambria*, although holder of the racing championship for coasters, was not the barge she was on match days and was sadly in need of a re-fit. Moreover, her skipper, Frank Tovell of Pin Mill, better known among the coasting fraternity as 'Cully', had at the time a mate who could not steer a much better course than something akin to a drunken snake. So to sail against her was not much of a test for us. In fact, although she undocked before us and had a long start we ramped past her off the North-east Gunfleet while her mate was laboriously trying to write his name in the last of the ebb.

The *Dannebrog* was a much different proposition. She got along well when before the wind and it had shifted to the east that day. Old 'Mo' King, another Pin Mill man, was master of her at the time and he had served his time in boomies out of Harwich in the hard old days. And when 'Mo' took it into his head to hustle a barge along he took some catching. The wind was fresh enough to whip up a few white horses and once we squared off up the East Swin I had thought that we would overhaul the *Dannebrog*. But it was one of those days when 'Mo' wasn't going to be caught. Just when we seemed to be gaining on him he went away from us again and by the time the ebb met us in Sea Reach and the wind fell away to a few paltry airs he anchored a good mile ahead of us. We mustered on the night tide and sailed on up to the sugar wharf at Silvertown but 'Mo' was in no hurry and did not pick his anchor up until the next day. So although we were first barge to report in we could not really take any credit for it. I was a little disappointed but the trip gave our gear a shake down and I could see a few alterations that were required.

While waiting our turn to unload we chucked our sprit up a link on the stanliff, thus giving the mainsail a higher peak, slacking off the collar lashing at the throat to keep the set of the topsail. Then we rove a lacing on the foresail just above the tack to hold it to the bottle screw on the forestay and thus keep a tighter foot. The mizzen mast was hove further forward and the leeboards brought closer to the side of the barge by driving iron bolts between the bars and the shackles on the toggles.

We went to Ipswich again and loaded sugar, but this time the weather was very bad with south-westerly gales blowing for days on end and all the other barges preferred to wait for better conditions. Most of them were wooden and they had to consider the risk of straining and leaking.

This time we got 183 tons into her and the extra weight stiffened her up for a fifty miles dead beat to London against a strong south-wester. We didn't see our lee rail for three tides but she was much more sure of herself when coming about in rough water than she used to be.

We continued in the East Anglian trade, ploughing to and fro throughout the winter with wheat from London to Norwich, sugar from Yarmouth and Ipswich for London, linseed from London to Ipswich, sulphate from London to Queenborough or Whitstable, cement from London to Colchester and occasionally export cement in the river from the Tunnel Works to big ships in the docks. But our most frequent passages were between London and Yarmouth, averaging a freight a fortnight and making enough money to cause the income tax man to cast covetous eyes on the rewards of our labours.

How the mate and I used to mutter grim curses on the Chancellor of the Exchequer when sloshing round Orfordness on a dirty night, dark and cold, struggling with a kicking wheel and dog-tired through lack of sleep, pulling and heaving and hoping for a chance to get a long delayed meal. On such a night I remember the mate being on the lee side of the wheel, weary and unshaven, up to his knees in water as she rolled and wallowed through the tide rip, saying with a voice full of vindictiveness:

'I wonder how much he'll take out of this lot?'

'I reckon he'll take the best part of it,' I replied. 'He might collar all of it seeing that we did the last freight in a week.'

'Well, if he wants a share of this the bastard ought to be here tonight and hold on to this bloody wheel.'

And he gave a vicious lug at the spokes to keep her away and then went on to bemoan the fact that we sometimes had to make a voyage for nothing to pay the tax on the previous two. That was if we hustled along with the work and got it done in the shortest possible time. If we dawdled we got slightly less money but a hell of a lot more time off. Some of the elderly bargemen used to do this and no one could blame them.

About this time, the war being over, a few lights began to appear on the buoys and there was less need for the lead line than had been the case in the previous six years. We used to creep down the Swin on dark nights by finding the edge of the Maplin Sands with the lead and then keeping in shallow water on that side of the channel until we judged that we were near the Whitaker Spit. Then it was up-helm and run north-east for three or four miles (according to the state of the tide) and then head north again until the lead fell on the edge of the Buxey. Thus we felt our way about something after the manner of a blind man groping for familiar objects.

It was all right in decent weather but when the gales were blowing we often sailed too close to the white water to feel comfortable in order to make quite sure where we were. Pencil and paper courses and theoretical navigation don't work out in the narrow channels of the Thames Estuary on winter nights. The slacks and eddies of the tide, the narrowness of the channels, the shifting sands and depths which change according to the wind, do not allow for the slightest error and there are places where a matter of a few yards one way or another can mean safety or disaster. But we had to do it to earn a living and the only alternative was to lie about and wait for fine weather and daylight tides. That was all very well but it sometimes meant taking weeks over a passage which could be made in a matter of twenty-four hours with a fair breeze. Anyway, it was good practice for foggy weather.

This reminds me of a Gravesend skipper who came driving up Swin one evening when it was not only getting dark but shutting in with thick fog. His mate, an argumentative fellow, was more worried than his skipper and thought with awe of the possibility of being set off into the steamboat channel in water too deep to anchor and perhaps running foul off the Nore Towers or being run down by a big ship. But the skipper, who was never one to be weighed down by anxiety, watched for the cut in the tide between the South East Maplin and the Blacktail Spit, took a cast now and then, watched the set and drift by slacking out twenty fathoms of lead line, and felt quite certain that he was going to anchor at the South Shoebury at high water or thereabouts.

Close astern of the barge came a naval patrol vessel. Presently Jimmy called out to his mate to stand by the anchor. Of course the mate must argue about it and said he thought they were too far off to let go.

'You do what I tell you and don't bloody well argue,' replied the skipper. 'Down foresail — let go. Give her fifteen in the water.'

Down went the anchor and the mate paid out the chain. Then he came aft again.

'Where do you think we are, skip?'

'Close by the South Shoebury buoy.'

46

'I reckon we're a good way outside that,' said the mate. 'It was a long time before our anchor touched the bottom and there ain't much of a lead on the chain.'

Just then the patrol boat loomed up on the quarter and gave then a hail.

'Barge ahoy! Where do you think we are?'

The skipper, fed up with being pestered about where he was when he was quite sure in his own mind, took off his cap, scratched his head and heaved a sigh. Then he answered the hail.

'Well, I reckon we're here, but my mate says we're further to the south'ard'.

And with that he went below to get his supper.

Straw Stack Trade

WHEN the winter weather tapered off and the pleasure boats and yachts began to appear to bear us company on our watery ways, a new job came along for us — and for many other barges too. It was carrying stacks of straw.

Owing to the shortage of wood pulp for making paper, machinery had been installed in the big mill near Sittingbourne to 'cook' straw into a white mash and use it instead of the pulp made from wood, rag or esparto grass. This straw came largely from the wheat fields of Essex and Suffolk and was brought in lorries to Hythe Quay (Colchester). There it was loaded into sailing barges and taken across the Estuary and up the Swale to Ridham Dock, which was a tidal dock owned by the mill.

In the old days stacks of straw and hay were taken to London in sailing barges for the horses who worked in the city streets. But in late years, the arrival of automobiles and the consequent eclipse of horse-drawn vehicles, caused the stack work to fall away to nothing. I had not seen a stack barge under way for something like ten years and even then she was an unusual sight. In fact, I believe the last one to come to London was in the winter of 1937.

Barges used to be specially built and rigged for the job so that they would sail quite well with the stack nearly half way up the mast. But when we came to revive the trade by loading pressed bales in Colchester there were few barges suitable for the work, and none less suitable than a heavily rigged coaster like the *Greenhithe*.

Much of the loading we had to do ourselves, assisted by the lorry drivers, most of whom were country chaps accustomed to stacking straw either in the fields or on their lorries.

Hythe Quay took on quite an agricultural air. Straw was littered all over the place and even floated up and down on the tide; one heard the slow, musical accent of the men from the fields and hedgerows; long handled stacking hooks and even pitchforks became the tools of the day; and the red sailed barges looked more like part of a farm scene than seagoing craft.

It was hard work at times but not unpleasant when the warm summer weather came along. Between the sweaty moments of pushing and shoving to get the bales tight together there were the more leisurely intervals of sitting on the straw waiting for the next lorry to come or falling asleep on top of the stack in the dinner hour.

Sometimes we would sit and swap tales of the barges for those from the farms. Occasionally a rat would come scuttling out of a bale of straw and all hands, young and old, would grab sticks and boathooks and go whooping round the barge in hot pursuit.

The first time we loaded straw we got $22\frac{1}{2}$ tons in the hold and then stacked thirty tons above the deck about ten feet high. In a proper stack barge this would run the full length between the main-horse and the fore coamings. The mainsail would be laced up to a specially provided row of eyelets half way up the sail, the foresail likewise, and the main brail taken off the crab winch by the mast and led forward to the dolly winch on the windlass bitt heads. But the *Greenhithe's* gear was too heavy to take advantage of these refinements and conveniences so we had to leave a hole in the stack so that the mate could get down to the winch.

On this winch were the foresail and topsail halyards and the main brail.

The mate used to call this the 'engine room' and sometimes he disappeared down there faster than he intended. If he was down in the 'engine room' I had to leave the wheel, climb the stack and shout down to him what sail I wanted set or lowered as the case might be.

To see where we were going was not quite so bad as one might imagine because when the barge was under way the wind and gear always listed her over and the helmsman could always peep round the windward side of the stack. Of course in narrow waters we had to have one man on top of the stack to direct operations and we soon developed a highly specialised form of 'tic-tac' signalling to the helmsman.

Of course the barge was very unwieldy to handle and an apt description of her abilities under this great bulk of straw was that she was like trying to sail a haystack. Sometimes she would come round and sometimes she wouldn't. It was worse still trying to bear up because as soon as the barge was well off the wind the breeze might catch the after corner of the stack and luff her back again against her helm. Then she would gradually lose way and lie with the wind abeam, completely unmanoeuvrable. On such occasions, which, fortunately, were very rare, we had to let go the anchor to chuck her round head to tide and then get her under way again as she took on the other tack.

When we used to sail into the Medway at Sheerness, clumsily threading our way between the destroyers and cruisers moored there, we made a fine butt for the wit and humour of the Navy's lower deck. Once we drifted into the mouth of the river in a flat calm, the first of the flood carrying us amongst all the mooring buoys and Naval ships and craft lying off Sheerness dockyard. In any other place the anchor would have been brought into use but here the bottom is interlaced with great chains and cables big enough to hold His Majesty's battleships. For us to have let go would have meant losing an anchor and chain.

Right in our path lay a great cruiser, her gangway and boat booms swung out, small craft alongside, and men on a staging painting down near the water line. Had we set fire to the straw we would have been the perfect imitation of an old fashioned fire-ship sent drifting among the fleet by some enemy lurking without.

Unwilling to lose my anchor and chain and unable to turn the barge one way or the other, we bore down on her and stood by ready for anything. In blissful ignorance the men on the staging overside continued with their painting and we missed them by about a couple of feet. But we did not miss the cruiser. Our stack, which overhung the sides of the barge by about three feet, brushed alongside her just forward of amidships and then all at once her crew sprang into action.

An officer rasped out orders and had a couple of dozen men tearing along the deck in a matter of a couple of seconds.

'Up gangway. In booms. Clear all craft.'

It was a smart piece of work. They got everything clear and we lumbered by, sweeping her sides and leaving wisps of straw hanging on her here and there. A forest of boat-hooks from her deck shoved us clear. In the presence of the officer there were no remarks, no laughter; everything was done in silence.

But just as we drifted clear of her stern an individual with a long neck and a solemn face poked his head out of a porthole and gave a long 'Moooooo'.

The worst job was getting through King's Ferry bridge, which crosses the Swale River near Ridham Dock. The bridge had a lifting span for vessels to pass and they normally employ the services of the local 'huffler'. There used to be more than a dozen of these 'hufflers' at King's Ferry in the hey-day of sailing barges and they all had enough work to do to earn a decent living. They took it in turns as the craft arrived and sometimes piloted them on up to the wharves in Milton Creek.

There is only one 'huffler' left now and he is getting on in years. The great stacks of straw dismayed him and he declared that if he could not see properly to judge his distance he would not take them through. This meant to us that if we were to load smaller stacks and lose several pounds freightage to suit the King's Ferry 'huffler' then the job was not worth doing.

So we had to get the local tug, if we could, and if the tug was not available we used to sail through ourselves without any assistance. One barge clouted the bridge and did some damage but generally we all wafted majestically through and heaved a sigh of relief as we emerged to the other side.

I remember one occasion when we came up the creek with a fair wind over the ebb and had stowed up the mainsail, using only the topsail and staysail to carry us to the anchorage where we generally waited for the slack or flood tide, according to weather conditions. I was rather surprised (being ebb tide) to see the opening signal go up on the bridgehouse and in a few moments the span began to lift.

I aimed for the bridgehole and had the mate slack out a bit of mainsail to help her along. We could not set all the mainsail because that would have obliterated my view altogether.

By the time we surged into the bridgehole and met the full sluice of the tide as it bottled between the buttresses we lost the wind under the lee of the bridge and began to drift out again. When far enough astern we caught the wind again and pushed half way through the bridge once more. Then we lost the wind and the performance was repeated.

This went on for some time, the bridgeman looking anxiously down upon us from his watch tower.

The bridge carries the main roadway to Sheerness and also the railway line from there to Sittingbourne and

Chatham. By the time we had occupied the bridgehole for twenty minutes or more a collection of buses, cars, lorries and a charabanc or two had accumulated on either side of the bridge. Soon a train was added to the waiting list.

People began to wonder what was happening and got out of their cars and buses to see what the matter could be. All they could see was a barge's topsail and an enormous stack of straw slowly moving backwards and forwards like a two-handed saw.

All this time I had to be very careful with the helm in case the barge should be set foul of the bridge and the time passed much quicker for me than for the people growing bad tempered and impatient in the various conveyances on the road and rail. Presently the bridgeman called out:

'You'll have to drop her out. I can't hold the bridge up any longer. You'll get me hung.'

'Down topsail.'

The barge, losing way, began to come astern once more, this time my intention being to allow her to drift clear of the bridge and anchor. But to hold her straight I had to keep the staysail set, for had a puff of wind caught the side of our cumbersome load she would have canted broadside to the tide and fouled the bridge.

Just as her head dropped back clear of the bridgehole the bridgeman began to lower the span. Before it was half way down a particularly hard puff came up the river, caught our staysail, and we went roaring back into the hole again.

'Hold it, hold it,' I shouted at the top of my voice, fearing that our masts would be taken out.

Out of the corner of my eye I saw the bridgeman rush to his levers. The mate, needing no warning from me, jumped down the forecastle hatch in case the spars should catch the bridge and come crashing down on top of him.

On went the barge. The bridge span stopped its downward movement and began slowly to go up again. I sheered

Barge up-country

the barge on to the side away from the lifting gear and gradually the space aloft widened.

'Topsail, up topsail,' I bawled; and I saw the agile figure of the mate come flying over the stack from forward and disappear down the 'engine room'. Slowly the great sail crept up the topmast. The freak puff whistled through the bridgehole and bellied out the heavy red canvas. The barge surged ahead, right through the bridge and out the other side. The span came down again.

For a few moments she hung there, just stemming the tide, and I heard the train and the road traffic roaring over just behind me. I was prepared to pull my helm up and shove her on to the mud for safety but the mate knew what to do without my telling him. He let go the brails of the mainsail and came charging up out of the 'engine room' to grab the mainsheet block and hook it on the wire lashing which went across the after end of the stack. I could not leave the wheel to help him but he got the canvas on her in record time so that as he slacked the weather vang we gradually gained ground and luffed round the corner into Ridham Dock.

'We've bin waitin' fer you,' one of the dockers said, 'our bloke said you was comin' up the creek an hour ago. Where you been?'

'Playing hide and seek,' said the mate with a grin as he took off the lashings and got ready to discharge.

As the straw work came along young Ken Fry, the third hand, left us to go mate with Jack Nunn in the *Princess* and later in the *Lady Maud*. He had done well enough aboard us to take the job and for his own sake I encouraged him to take the opportunity of learning all he could from such a fine old master.

'Perhaps you'll come back mate of the *Greenhithe* one day,' I said as I wished him luck. And sure enough he did.

Impromptu Races

IN the course of our voyages we occasionally found ourselves sailing in the company of the 270 tons barge *Will
Everard*; and as we were the only two purely sailing vessels
left who did any coasting to speak of there grew up a rivalry
between the crews which led to some impromptu and somewhat hectic races.

Sometimes we won; more often we were beaten. The *Will*
was so much bigger and longer and better designed that
she carried a spread of canvas amounting to 5,700 square
feet which could dwarf even the lofty *Greenhithe*. To windward the *Greenhithe* could not touch her and once the sheets
had to come in the big barge used to travel three feet to
our one and at least a point closer to the wind. Only with
the wind abeam or on the quarter could we hold her and
then sometimes only by carrying sail beyond the limits of
discretion. But we always had a go at her.

One day we were waiting to load flour for Lowestoft out
of a ship at the North Quay in the West India Dock when
the *Will* came blowing across the dock to load flour for
Yarmouth. Immediately an atmosphere of tension invaded
the workaday routine. There was a bit of banter and cross
talk between the mates about needing to polish the bottom
and grease the forefoot and some gratuitous advice on racing
staysails and reaching foresails.

These scraps of conversation seemed to interest a tall, bearded gentleman who stood about the *Will Everard's* deck and proved to be a commentator from the British Broadcasting Company. He was there to record what life was like aboard a sailing coaster — at least, such parts of it as were fit for the public to listen to. No doubt he thought that his little show would be livened up considerably by the prospect of a race against the *Greenhithe* for most of the way.

The *Greenhithe* was first to finish loading and as soon as the last bag was aboard and I had signed for the cargo and obtained my dock pass, we clapped the topsail on her and sailed through the cutting to the lock gates, the crew putting on hatches and getting ready for sea while I steered through the crowd of craft which assemble round the lock gates on the last of the flood tide.

The wind was easterly and we should need a start on the big barge if we were to keep her in sight at all. And of course my crew did not relish the idea of the B.B.C. gentleman crowing over the air on how the *Will* beat the *Greenhithe*.

Just before high water we undocked and a fitful breeze carried us clear of the lighters and out into Blackwall Reach. But no sooner were we out in the river than the wind fell right away and the *Greenhithe* lay like a log without a breath to fill her sails. Dead and motionless, she slopped the dirty water into her scuppers as the tugs and ships went by and as the minutes passed we knew that our advantage over the other barge was slipping away. Presently we saw her topmast coming away from the North Quay and it appeared that she was being towed round to the lock, the crew setting the canvas as she came.

A big Danube class tug had hold of her, giving her a friendly tow, and at the next lock-out she came out into the river, still under tow, while we lay still with our head turning slowly up river as she came surging past. The tug did not let her go until they reached the bend in the river which turns into Bugsby's Reach. Before she lost way the fitful breeze came back again and up went her huge staysail which set from her stem head almost up to her topmast head, a hundred feet above the deck.

Before we had gathered way under this new breeze — though still easterly — the *Will* was half a mile ahead of us, wriggling round the narrow bight into Woolwich Reach.

We were after her as soon as we had backed our headsails and got the *Greenhithe's* nose the right way, but as we sheeted home it was obvious that we had a lot of ground to make up. Our anticipated half hour start had been transformed into half a mile leeway and Jack the mate looked very glum.

'There goes my half quid,' he said mournfully, watching the *Will's* sails disappear round the sugar refinery. 'I bet Paddy we'd beat 'em to the Stanford Channel.'

(The Stanford Channel was where the barges would part company for their respective ports.)

Paddy, an Irishman who had been brought up as a fisherman out of Donegal, was mate of the *Will Everard*, and a very fine mate, too. His proper name was Hugh O'Donnell, but with a birthplace like Donegal and an accent as thick as an Irish stew it was hardly surprising that he was never called anything else but Paddy.

I told Jack that he must have more money than sense to back the *Greenhithe* to outsail the *Will* on a hundred and twenty miles beat to windward, and he looked glummer than ever. But the third hand cheered him up a bit when he said that all sorts of things might happen before we got to the Stanford Channel. The *Will* might sink, the skipper might die or the crew might mutiny — and in any case the B.B.C. bloke they had aboard might prove to be a Jonah.

All these possibilities, on being pointed out to the mate, saved him from the Well of Despondency and he set about his work with a better heart when we got a lucky puff round the back of some buildings and made up a bit of lost ground.

For lack of a third hand now that Ken Fry had gone we had shipped with us an old friend of mine who, although an amateur yachtsman, was a better hand than some of the lesser lights in the professional world. He had sailed boats from the time he could toddle and kept a smart little sloop at the Erith Yacht Club, so he was no stranger to London River. His name was Dave Kennard.

The *Will* was not at her best to windward without her bowsprit down and the great staysail she was carrying seemed to make her fall off the wind rather a lot after coming about as we tacked down the river. Whether it was this that allowed us to catch up on her or the fact that Jack kept muttering 'go on y'old bastard, get on with it' as he tended our sheets and leeboards, I do not know. More likely it was owing to the *Greenhithe* getting all the lucky puffs and the *Will* one or two unlucky ones, but we were tack and tack with her in Halfway Reach and finally caught her on the port tack. We winded quickly and stood towards her, we on the starboard tack. She stood on without a flutter, trying to stop us from getting across her head and for a few moments the two barges charged at each other like a couple of armoured knights in the lists.

The *Greenhithe*, being on the starboard tack, held right of way, but still the *Will* came on at us, trying to bluff me into giving way to avoid a collision. By the time the vessels were within a few yards of each other our stem had passed across the *Will's* head and I could see her wheel being put up spoke by spoke. At the last moment she bore away just a fraction and went under our lee. Her foresail shook as we took her wind and she began to slow up.

Round we came again smartly, almost on top of her, to hold her 'under our wing'. As we tacked together again on the south side of the river we spoilt her wind again.

From then on she could not catch us, and all the way down Erith Reach and Long Reach to the anchorage at Greenhithe we kept to windward of her and just saved our tide to the anchorage there. The *Will* just failed to do this and had to make several boards over the first of the flood and brought up about half a mile astern. But that was only the start.

The next day the wind was still easterly and there was no small amount of excitement on our shipyard and in the village when the two barges commenced to get under way. Everyone knew that a race was inevitable and many a workman put down his tools to see which one got the better start.

The *Will* lowered her bowsprit and set two jibs as soon as she was under way but in smooth water the *Greenhithe* did better with an inboard rig and the staysail on the stemhead. Down through St Clements Reach and Northfleet Hope we kept our half mile lead but as we worked down Gravesend Reach we began to lose the shelter of the narrows. The freshening wind was more to the liking of the big barge and she began steadily to overhaul us. Jack lowered our bowsprit and loosed the standing jib ready for the changeover. He could work fast when he was in the mind and in a matter of ten minutes (with the help of the third hand) he had got the thirty-four feet bowsprit rigged, set the jib, unbent the big staysail, bent it on the bowsprit end on the long topmast stay and set it up over the top of the standing jib.

By this time we were round the Ovens buoy and in the Lower Hope. The east wind flecked the ebb tide with patches of white and our lee decks began to carry a lot of water.

The *Will* crept nearer and nearer. Every time we crossed tacks she was closer to our stern. I could see that she was moving faster and more sweetly than we were and her lee deck was as dry as a bone. Our big staysail (now a jib topsail) was too much for her really but we hung on and buried our decks in a desperate effort to stave off the inevitable.

At last she came close up under our lee quarter and for a couple of tacks we blanketed her every time she tried to come by. But it could not go on for long, I knew. Presently she winded under our stern and romped away to the Essex shore like a racehorse. We winded and staggered after her but the next time she came about she was able to cross our bowsprit end with some fifty yards to spare.

We could see Paddy laughing as he trotted forward to tend his head sheets as she winded again to put us under her lee.

'We'll tell 'em you're coming,' he called out cheerily, and Jack muttered something inaudible under his breath as she clipped past us and left us astern. We made desperate efforts to hold close to her in the hope of forcing her into the slack tide but we were heeling rails under, over canvassed and carrying so much water on the lee deck that Dave was up to his knees in it when looking after the staysail sheets.

From then on every tack put us further and further astern until the flood came against us. Both barges were then compelled to anchor, being a little way beyond Southend pier, and the *Will* was about a mile ahead.

It was ten o'clock at night before the tide had eased sufficiently to get under way again and by this time there had been a slight change in the weather. The easterly bluster had fallen away to a gentle breeze from the south-east and the waters of the estuary were calm.

It was a black, moonless night and there was a host of steamboats coming out of Sea Reach. Unwilling to let the crew of the *Will* know that we were under way we did not ship any sidelights and made a long board to the southward in the hope of picking her up and surprising her while we were on the starboard tack.

For half an hour we saw no sign of her and we stood away to the north-east under every stitch of canvas we could set. Steamboatmen shouted and swore at us and we must have looked weird and ghostlike as we heeled silently between them. We were informed in no uncertain terms and with a considerable degree of rudeness that our lights were out, that we must be looking for trouble and that the barge was some sort of maritime lunatic. But I wasn't looking for trouble. I was looking for the *Will Everard*.

I had both hands forward straining their eyes into the inky darkness looking for the shadowy shape of our rival's sails.

'There she is.'

We all saw her at the same time. She came leaning out of the night barely a hundred yards away — and not a light showing! Not even her cabin light.

We had made up a lot of lost ground and we must have been the first under way. Once more the battle was on, tack and tack, wind and wind, neither barge willing to give away an inch or make a long board to seaward for the sake of safety and comfort.

After a time we were in such a position that both vessels were standing in towards the Shoebury Sands on the starboard tack, with the *Greenhithe* on the *Will's* lee quarter. Naturally the *Will* stood close to the sand to prevent us from sailing round her stern and getting the windward berth on the next board. Into the shallows we went with the lead line going — four fathoms, three, two and a half —.

It is steep here. I did not like the idea of it at all. Jack looked at me anxiously after every cast. I pictured both barges looking thoroughly ridiculous next daylight, perched up on a sandhill, a butt for the wit of all the other barges which happened to pass by.

'Two fathoms.'

'Lee O.'

Round we came, and filled away on the off-shore tack. There was more ebb stream farther out and by the time the *Will* was round I reckoned that she would be in the slack tide and lose a bit of her lead. Both barges had lights in now that we had discovered each other and we watched for the *Will's* green to appear when she winded so that we could judge if we were gaining on her.

But it never appeared. We heard someone shout. Her stern light disappeared and instead of the green the red port light came to view. This meant that she must have turned right round before the wind.

We stood in shore again and watched it carefully. Suddenly Jack threw his hat on the deck and did a dance of triumph.

'She's aground. She's on the Shoebury. She's up in the fields; stuck on bloody Essex!'

The mate's face was a picture. He almost let out a cheer. There is no question of Corinthian sportsmanship in these barge v barge affairs and he was as near bubbling over with joy as he could be at the other barge's misfortune. I felt sorry in a way for the skipper of the *Will* and knew well enough how he must have felt. Dave reckoned that probably the skipper and mate were by now fighting with hitchers on the main hatches or else taking it out of the B.B.C. beard. We wondered what their passenger thought of being stranded on the Shoebury Sands in the middle of the night when he was in process of recording the defeat of the *Greenhithe*. But he was not to be outdone for all that. In his subsequent broadcast he painted a thrilling picture of the *Greenhithe* being outsailed and outpaced by the *Will Everard*, our barge gradually falling astern, beaten and dispirited. There was no mention of his sojourn on the Shoebury Sands. Personally, I thought it would have made a much better story. As it was the *Greenhithe* was supposed to have been beaten to a frazzle and the whole tale lacked both honesty and truth.

What actually happened was that we picked up a smart south-east breeze next morning while the *Will* was still pretending to be a lorry and we rattled down the East Swin with two big jibs and a reaching foresail lugging us along at a fine rate of knots. The weather was as kind to us as it could possibly be and I doubt if the *Will Everard* would have caught us even if she had been afloat. Before it was dark again we were snugly moored in Lowestoft's inner harbour and ready to discharge our flour.

The broker's clerk came down to the quay and, his office being a branch of a Yarmouth firm, he asked if we had any news of the *Will Everard*.

The mate looked at him and grinned.

'He's still coming,' he answered with a wealth of meaning and a wink to me as he thrust his hand in his trousers pocket and jingled some loose coins.

Ten hours later the *Will Everard* sailed by on her way to Yarmouth, there to deposit the gentleman from the B.B.C. on shore to hasten to London with his graphic story of her 'victory' over the *Greenhithe*.

Humber Run

FOR close on a couple of years the *Greenhithe* was kept busy with cargoes from London. There was flour to Yarmouth and Lowestoft, wheat to Norwich, fertiliser to King's Lynn. On our way back with an empty barge we sometimes loaded raw sugar in Ipswich for Silvertown or straw in Colchester for Ridham. And when things were a bit quiet we occasionally did a freight of cement in London River from the works up to the docks. But when trade began to slacken seriously we had to look farther afield and started on a longer trek — to the Humber to load coal for Harwich and Colchester Gas Works.

Generally speaking, the prevailing south-west winds made the passage north fairly fast and comfortable; but slamming back deep loaded, against head winds half the time (sometimes all the time), is a very different matter. Jack the mate (my small daughter always thought that his proper name was Jack the Mate — like Jack the Giant Killer and other worthy characters) got fed up with the continual drenchings, and every time we passed through Yarmouth Roads he would look at the chimney pot of his home ashore there and think of all the cosy comforts therein.

He was always grimly cheerful about it but the pull to go ashore for good grew stronger when he began to contemplate matrimony.

Before he finally packed up the sea and went on land to prosper as a painter and decorator, he helped me to make some pretty good passages.

On one occasion in particular we sailed from Yarmouth empty bound for Keadby (up the River Trent) and averaged eight knots from the pierheads to Hull Roads. Everything was in our favour. The barge was clean, there was a fresh southerly wind, and at no time did we have to punch the full strength of the tide. After we had crossed the 'deeps' between Burnham Flats and the Lincolnshire coast and made our landfall near Mablethorpe we found that the tide was slack and by the time we rounded Donna Nook to go up the Humber the flood had just started.

As we ran past the trawler fleet lying off Grimsby the mate stowed the jib, steeved up the boltsprit and set the staysail on the stem head. Tides run swiftly in the Humber and as there was no sign of the Keadby tug in Hull Roads we hauled our sheets a little and laid away up the river, past Reed Island and round the dangerous Whitton Sand which squats obstinately in the middle of the river and stretches almost from bank to bank, leaving a narrow U shaped channel running round the northern side of it. Off the mouth of the Trent the wind began to fall light and there were the usual flights of anxiety until we were safely in the right river and being set up past the new sea wall at a hair-raising speed. There is always a risk that in calms and light airs a barge might be set by the flood tide up the River Ouse (for at this point the Trent and the Ouse meet to form the Humber). Capt Farrington, master of the Alaric, told me that when he had the coaster *Gertrude May* he was once being towed to Keadby on a strong spring tide and the tow rope broke in the hubble-bubble of tide where the rivers meet. The tug went up the Trent and his barge went up the Ouse and by the time he got under tow again he was nicely on his way to Goole!

Keadby itself is only a village — a row of cottages, three pubs and a coal shute. Two of the pubs are right by the coal jetty and so you can guess that they are well patronised by mariners seeking some small relief from their daily business on board. The people of Keadby are a hard working, friendly folk and they know some of the older coasting seamen almost as well as their own neighbours. It is a pleasant feeling when one goes ashore there to be welcomed as an old friend.

The loading is done by running the coal truck on to the shute, which lowers down to an angle sufficient to let the coal tip into the ship's hold as the end is knocked out of the truck. Like a black avalanche, nine or ten tons of coal comes hurtling down into the barge and the local trimmers scramble down amongst it to shovel it into the wings and 'cupboards' where it won't run on its own. They work hard, these trimmers, and it was very rarely that we came away from Keadby with less than 168-170 tons in us, and it is reckoned as light coal there, which takes up a lot of room. They earn good money while the ships are there — nothing when they have gone.

It took about two hours to put 170 tons into the *Greenhithe* and on the next day's tide the tug *Waterman* took us down to Hull Roads. We anchored there for the night and from then on our luck changed.

Hull Roads is not exactly a beauty spot and I never did think much of it as an anchorage. For a sailing barge, one has to lie too close to the shore to feel comfortable even in fine weather, and the swift running tide makes it difficult to get to and from the shore for stores, pints of beer, and all those things which go to make up a bargeman's life.

I was, therefore, anxious to bid farewell to the River Humber as soon as possible. Being bound to Harwich we needed a north-west breeze; but the previous day it had blown almost a gale from the southward.

About five o'clock in the morning I rolled out of my bunk and went on deck to see the prospects of the day.

Being July it was daylight then, and I could see the clouds bowling across the river from about west-south-west but there was rain and thunder over the Lincolnshire coast.

I called all hands and up came the mate out of the forecastle. There were only the two of us for we had not been able to get a third hand before we had sailed from London. Young lads born into a world of speed and comfort aren't too keen on sailing vessels these days.

We had a cup of tea and got under way on the high water at six o'clock. While we were heaving up there was a sharp shower of rain followed by a real downpour just as we shaped away down past Salt End and were getting the boat in the davits. So before we were properly started we were both pretty well wet through, for two hands cannot do all the work required in getting a 180 tons barge under way if they are dressed up in oilskins. And I never knew a bargeman to have a decent set of oilskins anyway. The usual outfit for wet weather is an old raincoat which has generally seen its best days ashore.

As we stretched away down by Grimsby the wind backed to the south-west and the wireless forecast was 'west to south-west; squally; thunder showers'.

There was little doubt that we were in for a dirty passage and there were one hundred and fifty miles of sailing to be done, so we had a mighty breakfast and innumerable cups of coffee before the old *Greenhithe* poked her nose round the Bull Sand Fort.

Once out of the river we hauled her on the wind and it wasn't long before the head of the topsail had to come down to ease our lee rail out of the water. With boltsprit jib, foresail, mainsail, mizzen and the sheet of the topsail, she bounced and sloshed her way round Ross Spit and was holding up well over the ebb to windward of the Inner Dowsing.

We knew we were going to have a washing going across the Deeps, but once under the lee of the land along by

Brancaster and Wells things should be a little more comfortable.

It was not pleasure trip. If I had been in a yacht I would have turned back. The rain was almost continuous and there was plenty of salt water swilling round the wheelhouse as she lay down on her ear in the harder puffs. East Coast sailors, whether they be amateur yachtsmen or professionals, know how much freeboard a loaded barge enjoys and in bad weather we often resemble a half tide rock. But as my old skipper used to say when I first went mate of a coasting barge, 'So long as you can see both ends and the topsail you're all right.'

So we kept her at it and were getting well to windward by the time the young flood began to help her along. We were almost out to Burnham Flats when a great black thunder cloud became visible to the southward and seemed to hang stationary for half an hour or more. I wondered whether it was wind or rain but for a long time it did not come near us. Then I could see rain sweeping down to earth behind it and a line of white water out to windward. The topsail being already down, we held on a little longer before taking off any more canvas, but seeing the white crests to the south we stowed the mizzen and I held her a point free ready to bear up should the squall be fierce.

It was!

It hit us with astonishing suddenness. I shoved the wheel up and the barge was coming off the wind when a cross sea hit her on the starboard quarter and forced her stern round against her helm. The *Greenhithe* took a root to windward just as the line of white water was upon us. It seemed like a hurricane. Over she went, down, down, until her lee hatch coamings were under water.

The mate rushed to the other side of the wheel.

'Up helm, up!' I yelled, and together we struggled to get the wheel over so that the vessel could run off before the wind. It is a dangerous thing to luff a barge in such

69

circumstances, for she may lose way and as she fills again she may be knocked flat. She must be kept moving.

By now that barge was hove over so far that half her lee decks and hatchway were underwater and the seas were swamping her from the lee side. Never before or since have I been in any vessel pressed down to such an angle as the *Greenhithe* was then. If a hatch had come off or if the flushing boards of the forecastle and cabin scuttles had not been in she would have filled up and sunk. The port light board, which is set in iron stanchions six feet above deck level, washed out and floated away. The tow rope, coiled down on the fore hatches, the highest part of the barge, came floating aft like a boa constrictor and wound itself round the mizzen rigging. Seas were swamping her from the lee side and she began to lose way. It was evident that she was not going to bear up. There was only one thing to do before she 'laid down and died'.

We had to get the weight of water off her decks. To do that we must down-helm and trust to Providence that she would bear up after that. The wind was howling like a horde of devils. There was another squall coming.

'Down helm.'

Slowly her head lurched into the seas and the water poured over her lee quarter. Various odds and ends floated out into the North Sea like flotsam on a Thames ebb.

By the time the barge had come close on the wind and assumed a fairly reasonable angle she had lost way and lay there like an Aunt Sally in a fair waiting to be knocked over.

For a few seconds we could only wait for it but the suspense made those seconds seem like half an hour. Then it came, a mighty blast, almost as hard as the one that had put her down. She literally staggered as a tired boxer would on taking a second hard punch. But she did not go down. Slowly she gathered way and once more we pulled the wheel hard up. This time she fell off far enough to take the full force of the wind just abaft the starboard beam — and all was well.

Away she went out to sea at about nine knots, over the top of the Race Bank and outside the Dudgeon; safe as houses but going like a train in the wrong direction. All our good work to windward earlier in the day was lost in an hour or so.

Just as we reached the Dudgeon Shoal there came the rain. It was so thick that we could hardly see the mast. Everything was blotted out. Although we were partly protected by the wheelhouse the water ran down inside our clothes as though we hadn't any on.

Then, as suddenly as it came, it petered out. Almost before we could realise it the rain had cleared and the wind dropped almost to a calm, leaving us rolling in a smooth topped swell.

As we drew breath and shook the water from our clothes I noticed a dark patch on the water to the north-west. I watched it for a moment and saw little ripples on the top of the swell.' It was a north-west breeze. We manned the crab winch and the topsail went up in double quick time. It was nearly two hours since she had been first hove down and here was the reward for all our labour and anxiety. A fair wind; God's greatest gift to sailormen.

All the rest of that day we bowled along by Sheringham and Cromer and when Jack had everything on deck ship-shape again he took the wheel and burst into his Fair Wind Song. This was not really a song at all, it was a dreadful, toneless dirge which went on hour after hour, quite unapplicable to favourable weather, and told the awful tale of a girl who hung herself because of the unfaithfulness of her seaman lover. But Jack always sang it when there was a fair wind so we hung her several times before we left Cromer astern and sailed along the sandy shore to Haisborough.

As night came the wind fell light and backed to the south-west again. We fetched a little way over the ebb but had to bring up at one o'clock in the morning in Hemsby Hole. We had been hard at it without a breather for nineteen hours.

We spent the last three hours of the ebb in our bunks and then set off again on a dead plug to windward against a moderate south-west wind. We hove the anchor up at four o'clock in the morning and by the time it was high water we were off Sizewell Gat. There the anchor had to go down again as the ebb came away.

The wind was off the land at the time and we were just settling down for an hour or two's well earned rest when the wind backed southerly, sending a short, sharp popple along the shore. The sky looked threatening and, being only two handed, I thought we had better get out anchor while we could in spite of the fact that we were getting very tired.

For the last two hours of the ebb we had to bang to and fro, losing ground to the ebb until low water, by which time we were back off Southwold.

Had the wind been more westerly we might have reached Harwich on that flood but it turned out to be one of those breezes that would make a saint swear, let alone a weary bargeman. Once or twice we got a long leg but sometimes we were east on one tack and west on the other.

We got her round Orfordness and up as far as the Cutler before the tide was done. It was then dark and we could see the glow of the shore lights round Harwich and Felixstowe. But the ebb came away as we stood in towards Bawdsey Cliffs and I could see that the Cork Lightship had swung.

The wind freshened and it started to rain hard. We hoped that the rain would make the wind fly north-west — but it was a forlorn hope. That is why we kept under way. But the rain belonged to that south-west wind and we got both of them in increasing quantities. Enough sea got up to break over our bowboards and wash the anchor chain back as far as the fore-horse. It was certainly not fit to bring up and she would only have parted her cable, so we *had* to keep her under way.

It blew so hard that we had to drop the head of the topsail down and by midnight there was a moderate gale in

operation. It looked as though we might have to run back
to Yarmouth Roads for shelter. Seeing the lights of Harwich
and then having to run back was more than we had heart
to do, so we kept plugging away until a heavy sea pitched
into the boltsprit jib. The mate, tired, wet and fed up,
hauled down the remains and I hove her to under foresail
and full mainsail.

As she edged off to Bawdsey Bank we went below and
made some cocoa. With the foresail aback she did not need
anyone at the helm. We used to lock the wheel about
amidships and let her get on with it, taking turns to keep
watch from the shelter of the cabin scuttle. When she was
near enough to Bawdsey Bank we let draw, put her round
on the other tack and let her lie on her bowline again.

Low water was at daylight and by that time we were back
off Orfordness again — cold, tired out and wet through. It
was the most miserable night I have ever spent aboard a
barge. Only one thing saved us from utter despondency. I
suddenly remembered that Dave Kennard (our occasional
passenger-cum-third-hand) had always made a practice of
bringing a bottle of rum with him to 'pay his dues' as he
used to say. In my locker were the remains of one of these
priceless gifts — only about six inches in the bottle — but
what a find that was.

Jack said he didn't like rum; but he did that night. We
put boiling hot water with it and the pair of us glowed with
fresh endeavour as daylight broke and the flood tide started
to flow again.

We re-commenced our plug to windward, but with no
jib and a heavy sea still running our progress was far from
spectacular. For some time it was doubtful whether she
would carry her flood far enough to fetch round the Beach
End, but she did it, thank Heaven, and we went sorting
into the harbour like a greyhound.

The berth where we were to discharge is a creek alongside
the Gas Works, and in it fishing boats moor on condition

that they leave room for vessels to come to and from the coal quay. It was high water and I was determined to finish the job on that tide.

In went the barge through the narrow gut that leads into a sort of cul-de-sac, with the bowsprit still down (for the mate had not had time to top it up) and all sail set to hold her up against the eddy coming down the south shore of the Stour. The berth was cluttered up with fishing craft and small boats. As they saw us coming there was a frantic letting go of ropes and a panic-striken flight out of the small boats which could not be pulled out of the way in time.

The mate got the sail off her just in time and as the *Greenhithe* ranged alongside the quay a friendly soul lobbed our best mooring rope over the one and only bollard there while I locked the wheel and caught a turn round the main-horse.

For a moment I thought we were going to wipe one or two little boats off the face of the earth. There was no room to surge the check rope to avoid breaking it so it squeaked and groaned but held on. The barge stopped dead in her berth. I ran forward to help Jack get a head rope out and to see if we had damaged any of the open boats. Everything was all right; but under our boltsprit an old man, not so active as the rest, stood crouching in a little skiff waiting for the fatal crunch which would end his life.

'All right dad,' I called out to him, 'we're all stopped. You can stand up now.'

Everyone breathed again and the old man smiled at me admiringly.

'I can see you've done that job a-fore, skipper,' he said, little suspecting that I was just as relieved as he was!

We cleared the decks, took the cloths and hatches off and got ready to discharge. After dinner the mate turned in and I went home, leaving the dockers to get on with the job. We'd done ours.

I took the missus to the pictures that night and watched American he-men heroes diving through sixty foot waves, fighting off sharks and rescuing beautiful blondes from death and dishonour. It was all very exciting — real adventure stuff. The Race Bank and the Dudgeon Shoal and the old barge being hove over on her side seemed a long way off, like something unreal in another world. Besides, that was only work whereas this film affair was full of real thrills.

Not long after this Jack left the barge. We had just unloaded flour at the A.B.C. wharf in Yarmouth and he went off to set up his own business. I was sorry to lose him. He was a good little sailorman. There is no need for me to say more.

After he went I had a couple of short-term mates. One of them, a young man named Hazelton from Ipswich, was a particularly smart seaman but he only came with me for three months while waiting to go skipper of a small barge named the *Saltcote Belle*. He was very young to take charge of a barge — only 18 — but he did fairly well in spite of one or two unlucky accidents.

Gale in the Wash

<hr />

I HAD been to the city for orders one day and was making
a short board across Fenchurch Street in the direction of the
East India Tavern when I was almost run down by a
straight, square shouldered figure with a ruddy countenance
who was none other than my old friend Capt Bert Fry of
the motor ship *Audacity*.

He still had a bargeman's ways about him and he bore
up sharply so that I could not get clear of him and we both
landed up inside the pub.

'Bit o' luck, Bob,' he commented. 'They were just
locking in. Where you for?'

'Norwich. Wheat for Read's.'

We drank beer and yarned for a little while and then I
asked after his son Ken, who had been my third hand when
the *Greenhithe* was re-fitted.

'He's eating his heart out in the *Prowess*.'

The *Prowess* was a little motor tanker.

'Well, I want a mate,' I said. 'Would he come back with
me.'

'I don't know. Is he good enough for mate?'

I nodded. Bert gave me details of how to get in touch
with him and then hurried off to catch his train to Gravesend.
If Ken had been good enough as mate for old Jack Nunn
he was good enough for me. So I sent him a letter and a

telegram and then got on with my business of loading 800 quarters of wheat in bulk out of a steamship in the Victoria Dock.

Hazelton did the trip with me and we also had with us young Jim Godfrey from Ipswich, a little lad whom he had helped along in hard times. Jim stayed on as third hand for some time and eventually became mate of a barge named the *Alice May*.

We had an easy roll down to Yarmouth. The wind was southerly and not too strong and there was only enough swell to keep the midship decks swilled. Tides were lazy that week and as we came into Gorleston Roads we hauled our sheets and sailed her between the pierheads and right up to the Town Quay. The next morning the little tug *Cypress* took us in tow for the six hours trip up the Yare and after a week-end up there she lugged us back to Yarmouth again. Here Hazelton went off to take his new command and the following day the burly figure of Ken Fry jumped aboard.

He had changed a bit since first being with me as third hand. He was bigger and stronger, more confident and more efficient. The businesslike way he set about things aboard bore a marked resemblance to his father.

Ken had one great quality — whenever he set out to do something it was obvious from the start that he was going to get it done. No half measures; no thought of failure — he refused to be baulked by anything or anybody if a job had to be done. Sheer tiredness would never stop him. When sometimes we arrived at our port of destination after a rough passage and sleepless nights at sea he would never rest or take off his wet clothes until he had cleared the hatches, knocked the wedges out, hauled the sprit to one side, coiled everything down neatly, seen to the moorings and made all ready to discharge. Then he would sit down to a cup of tea with no more comment than 'Rough passage, skip.'

He was a sailor all right. He couldn't help it. It was born in him. [Under the remarkable modern organisation of our daily lives by people who do not know anything about us he was eventually compelled to be come a soldier!]

One day we were unloading straw at Ridham when we had orders to proceed to the Surrey Dock and load fertiliser for King's Lynn. This job was not entirely unwelcome because trade was getting very slack and the straw business looked like drawing to a close.

We had only been to Lynn once since the end of the war. Not that I was a great lover of this back o' beyond port except in that it had a history which went back to Saxon and Roman times, or even before that. I always understood that the word Lynn was of ancient Celtic origin and meant a lake or large expanse of water, just as London probably gets its name from 'Lynn Dun' — a fort by the lake. A 'Dun' was a fortified place probably surrounded by earthworks and palisades to keep out both human enemies and wild beasts.

Writing of King's Lynn always reminds me of a famous old coasting skipper named Freddie Bridger, who used to be master of the boomie *Evelyn* and later the *Will Everard*. He was a bluff, hard living sailorman of the old school and even in the days when there was more leisure in business than there is now he made some remarkable passages, never daunted by wind and weather.

He had been in a regular trade of carrying oilcake from London to King's Lynn for several months, and when one Friday he had just finished loading in the Millwall Docks he saw that there was a fresh breeze from the south-south-west.

'Get those hatches on, Mister Mate, get her all ready. We'll lock out tonight. With a wind like this we'll be there for Monday morning's work.'

The mate bustled round and out went the *Evelyn* into the blackness of the night. Before long she was squared off for what Freddie reckoned was going to be a quick passage. So it was. On Sunday afternoon the Lynn pilot boarded him at Bar Flat. (There was a different channel into Lynn in those days.)

'We weren't expecting you skipper,' the pilot said. 'Which wharf are you for?'

'Go to hell if I know,' said Freddie. 'We came away all of a rush and tear and I didn't find out. Hold on to this wheel a minute and I'll nip down below and have a look at my Bill of Lading.'

When Freddie came up on deck again (the pilot told me some years after) his face can only be described as blank astonishment. He looked stunned.

'What's the matter skipper?' Asked the pilot, sensing that something had gone wrong.

Freddie coughed and swallowed hard. He found it difficult to speak. At last he blurted out the awful truth.

'We ain't for Lynn at all. We're for Poole.'

And he waved the incriminating Bill of Lading in the pilot's face. He pushed the pilot away from the wheel and spun the helm hard down.

'Lee oh. Fish that anchor up on the bow again. Blast, damn and hell — — — — .'

The next two chapters could, if legally permissible, be taken up with what Freddie Bridger said on that occasion. He could always swear. This came from him as naturally as roars from a lion. In fact they were very much like roars from a lion.

When the fury of his feelings had simmered down he got rid of the Lynn pilot, stood off to sea again and fetched Yarmouth Roads on the starboard tack. There the gods looked kindly upon him for the wind shifted to the north and he finally made Poole in reasonable time.

Whether the owners or the merchants ever knew that the oilcake had been to Lynn before it arrived in Poole I do not know. But Capt Bridger always took care to look at his Bill of Lading after that!

There is another story of this grand old sailorman. He once had a mate who said little but had a sense of solemn humour. His lanky body, his lean, sad face and slow speech were rather typical of his character.

They had been down to the West Country to load china clay and once nicely clear of the land she rolled away up-Channel with a strong south-west wind. The weather looked bad and there was every prospect of a gale coming on before next daylight. Freddie had his crew crack on every stitch she would bear, for a south-westerly gale to him was a blessing to be thankful for not a thing to be afraid of.

When the barge was trimmed on to her long course the mate was called to the wheel. Freddie turned in. He always turned in when there was a clear run and nothing to worry about.

The wind blew harder. By nightfall the mate and third hand were one each side of the wheel, lugging this way and that, trying to steer a reasonable course as she rushed madly to the eastward. Presently, after a heavy rain squall, the melancholy mate went below and knocked on the skipper's cabin door.

'What's the matter?'

'Skipper; comin' on to blow. Reckon we ought to have that topsail down out of it.'

Freddie was out of his bunk in a moment. It was no small thing for anyone to suggest taking sail off his barge when there was a fair wind. He poked his head out of the scuttle hatch, sniffed contemptuously at the weather and looked aloft. It certainly did look threatening. But it was against Freddie's grain to take that topsail in.

'Moon'll be up presently,' he said. 'Moon'll eat the wind up. Always does. Never so much wind when the moon gets up. Eats the guts out of the wind.'

And without giving permission for the topsail to be taken in he went below again.

It blew harder and harder. An hour or so later the mate once more dared to rouse him with a brief request to be allowed to get the topsail off her.

'Is the moon up yet?' said Freddie without even troubling to look out.

'Not yet, skipper. But its blowin' a gale o' wind now. Fair hummin' it is. Much as we can do to steer her.'

'Hang on a bit longer. Moon'll soon eat the wind up.'

So back went the mate to renew his struggle at the wheel but not long after there was an onmious rending sound from aloft. The topsail had started to go. Before the crew had a chance to do anything or even call the skipper it split from head to leech and was soon nothing more than a bunch of ribbons streaming out to leeward.

For a few moments the mate regarded the chaos aloft. Also he saw that the moon had risen in the east.

'Hold this wheel a minute Joe,' he said to the third hand in his ponderous rural dialect.

Down the cabin steps he went once more with a measured tread and there was a faint touch of triumph as he knocked on the door.

'Moon's up now, skipper — but it ain't ate the wind up, its bin an' ate our tawps'l up.'

Freddie no longer contended that the moon eats the wind up at night. He's dead now but the tale of his topsail will never die as long as there are sailormen to tell it in the riverside taverns by the lower reaches of the Thames.

The fertiliser we had to load in the Surrey Dock was in bulk, as was usual these days. It was extremely heavy — about the same weight as cement. This was a good sailing cargo for the *Greenhithe* because being so cranky in a breeze she needed plenty of weight in her bottom to hold her at a tolerable angle in a fresh wind.

It was Easter time and to coasting tradition the weather was easterly. I once knew a bargeman who thought that Easter was so called because of the winds that prevailed at that time of the year! He knew more about weather than religion.

There was enough wind to whip up whitecaps in Gravesend Reach even on the lee-going tide so I felt that it was prudent to have patience and bide our time. Four days we lay in the river and in that time our crew gradually increased from two to five. Ken had urged his young cousin into the job of third hand and we were also joined by my young nephew on holiday from school and Dave Kennard (our amateur yachtsman — occasional bargeman — deputy third hand). So we stretched away down Gravesend Reach with such a crowd of people on deck (not forgetting the dog Susan who was a regular member of the crew) that we looked more like the Royal Eagle pleasure boat than an old barge bound to sea.

Our visitors had the very weather they might have wished for. It was warm and sunny and there was a nice sailing breeze from the south-south-east. By nightfall we were tearing away down the East Swin under mainsail, topsail, foresail jib and mizzen. The *Greenhithe* was not much cop to windward but she was no fool with a fair wind and there was nothing she liked better than a big jib on the boltsprit end. The mizzen had to come off her as we bore away round the North-east Gunfleet buoy but it took a long time for the steamboats to get by us between there and Orfordness. Two small motor coasters, who we reckoned were also bound to Lynn with phosphate, actually trailed away astern and did not catch us up again until the wind eased the following day off the Corton Lightship. That day we were literally dancing along through sunlit seas off Yarmouth and the harbour tug *George Jewson* came out thinking that we were bound there. 'If we had been we wouldn't have seen him for a couple of hours or more,' commented the mate. But it was too good a day to grumble about anything and we waved them a cheery goodbye as the skipper wished us a pleasant passage.

It was a grey afternoon and the sky began to look greasy. Our south-east wind veered to south and there came a drizzle of rain. There were some heavy puffs off the towering cliffs of Cromer and I feared that our good weather had come to an end.

About tea time we ran past Wells Bar and through Brancaster Road and I decided to find my way through the Woolpack sledway into the Wash to obviate going seven miles off to leeward and round the end of Burnham Flats. This sledway is narrow, shallow and unmarked but since by the time we approached it the wind had increased to almost a gale it was fairly easy to pick out the deep water. All the shoals showed white and we went in between the patches of broken water. It is not a passage for a stranger to tackle but I knew it fairly well, having been through there a dozen times before.

When we came out into the Wash we were fighting the ebb tide and although we hauled our sheets we could not quite fetch the Lynn Well Lightship. There was more sea in the Wash than I had expected but with three helmsmen aboard I thought it would not be a great hardship to keep under way and punch the ebb for some three hours, even though it was now blowing hard from the south-south-west. There was too much sea to bring up, so we banged to and fro between the Long Sand and the Woolpack, sometimes holding our own, sometimes gaining a little, sometimes losing ground. All the time the sea was increasing and the head of the topsail had to come down. Under mainsail, topsail sheet, foresail and jib she was beginning to stagger a bit as she winded and I knew that if any more sail had to come off her she would not come round for certain.

I did not fancy going back through the Woolpack with a loaded barge at low water in such weather (it was just a mass of white as darkness fell) and had we tried to run round Burnham Flats she would not have punched far enough to windward to get under the lee of Holkham and ride out the gale to an anchor. But I did think that as the tide began to flow we could get far enough to windward up the Wash to lie under the lee of the sands.

I was wrong and our luck was out.

The seas grew bigger and bigger. The wind blew harder and harder. By the time the tide was turning it was blowing a full gale with all the usual accompaniment of seas breaking over the main hatches, spray flying in the wheelhouse, water squirting through the leaky port holes into the cabin and soaking everything (including my bunk), crockery broken, meals uneaten, and all the time the unending battle with a kicking wheel. I got no joy out of it. I had had my share of all that.

When the flood tide came we were about two miles north-east of the Lynn Well Lightship but our progress to windward was next to nothing. Every time the old barge picked up a bit of way she was knocked silly by the steep seas. The mate, who was wet to the skin lashing things down while the others helped me at the wheel, came aft and reported that the jib had started to go. Down it had to come, just as it split up the leach, and the mate struggled out on the boltsprit footrope to stow it. Once when her head dipped down he was up to his shoulders in water. I ran forward to see if he was all right and he grinned cheerfully as he shot up out of the sea hanging on to the topmast stay for dear life. It was then that I noticed that the boltsprit had a queer angle to it and in a flash I realised that it was sprung at the stem head.

'Get aboard', I shouted.

'What about the jib,' he hollared back, for he was never a lad to shirk a job that had to be done.

'To hell with the jib. Leave it. Get aboard quick.'

He guessed that something was wrong and scrambled in along the footrope like a monkey, in spite of being cluttered up with oilskins. I told him to heave the jibstay as tight as he could and hurried back to the wheel. By the time I had grabbed hold of it again the barge had run off the wind and a sea pitched into the bellying remains of the jib. From then on we had no jib.

Daylight was almost gone and I hove the barge to, letting her lie on the bowline long enough to cross the mouth of the Wash, allowing ample room to get her round on to the other tack. But the seas were so steep by then that several times she missed stays and I felt it in my bones that we should not see Lynn that tide, or the next.

The gale was worse than ever as night fell and, being deep loaded, the spray flying across the barge almost blotted out the Lynn Well light. I had been sizing up the situation for the last couple of hours and reluctantly came to the conclusion that the only sensible thing left to do was to run for it. It was obvious that she would not punch up the Wash under such conditions and I did not want to risk losing any more sails, especially the mainsail and foresail, which was all she would bear.

To keep the sails intact was, therefore, my first consideration, for by so doing we would live to fight another day. So I ordered the main brail to be hove up and the mainsail all but stowed with the hook still on the traveller. Under foresail and the sheet of the topsail I put the helm hard up and ran her off to the north-east.

There was only one place we could run to for shelter and that was the Humber. That was about fifty miles to leeward; fifty miles farther on than we wanted to go.

We had been within five miles of a safe anchorage under the sands of the Wash and it was heartbreaking now to find ourselves being forced out into the open sea. After 150 miles of sailing we could not make the last five.

Things were more comfortable jogging along with the wind and sea astern and we were able to make tea and have something to eat. I even risked putting on a dry shirt so as to enjoy what small comfort is possible when standing at the wheel of a barge all night in a gale of wind, the second night to come and go without rest or sleep. What would some of your steamboat sailors say if they had to do forty-eight hours on deck without a break? Bargemen do not like doing it;

but they can stick it when they have to. Sailing on a share basis they are mainly interested in getting the vessel to her destination in the quickest possible time, getting the cargo discharged and getting another one loaded. The hours on deck and the work involved are matters of human endurance rather than regulations when bad weather comes on.

Young Ken's old grandfather would have been proud of him if he had seen that lad that trip. Never once during the gale did he leave the deck or ask for a spell below. He defied every sea that tried to wash him overboard as he went about his various tasks without a word of complaint and without waiting to be told what to do. It seemed as if in the storm he had grown from boy to an old sea-dog, as familiar with salt water as a shepherd is with grass.

I can see him now in the gathering gloom bending over one of our mooring ropes that had washed into the scuppers, carefully coiling and lashing it down, several times almost hidden by spray and the weather water swirling round him as it cascaded down to leeward. He was neither flurried nor hurried and every task he set about was duly accomplished. Nothing was allowed to carry away. Every item on deck was accounted for. Even a small ball of spunyarn which came floating along the lee deck was carefully retrieved and hung up in the wheelhouse to dry.

A Viking lad indeed. And it was left to the Gods of the Storm to bring out his real worth. He reminded me very much of an elderly Dane I once knew in an old barquentine laying down the law to a Cornishman on the best way to grow tomatoes while they struggled up to their waists in water to tend the lee brace.

We ran fifty miles to the Humber, still under foresail and topsail sheet only, in eight hours, so that when daylight came the *Greenhithe* was reaching in over Haile Sand Flat, the wind having westered and blowing like the devil. The Humber entrance was a mass of foam and the trawlers off Grimsby had so much cable out that they were half way across the river.

86

We stretched away up as far as Sunk Island, wore her round with a scrap of mainsail slacked out in the brails, and finally came to anchor in three fathoms in Grimsby Roads. Her hook bit into the clay and we gave her thirty fathoms of chain before going below to strip off, eat and sleep.

The elements continued to bluster and rage for another two days and then, with a light westerly breeze and smooth water, we commenced to wend out way back to Lynn.

We had fine weather, thunder squalls and finally torrential and continuous rain, so that all the salt in our clothes was washed out and we arrived in King's Lynn as clean and spruce as a ship and crew could be.

The phosphate out, a new bowsprit and jib arrived for us on a lorry, and it was not long before we were coasting back to the Humber again to load coal at Keadby for Harwich.

The trip home with the coal was not exactly a holiday and we ran an easterly gale from Yarmouth Roads to the Cork; but we did the round trip in less than a fortnight so that there was a fairly handsome profit — at least we thought so until the income tax man put his hand out for his share (although I had not noticed him on deck that night off the Wash).

Race to Yarmouth

ONE day we came sailing down London River on the last of the ebb with a 165 tons of Canadian flour for the A.B.C. wharf at Yarmouth. It was springtime and the winds were fickle and we anchored for the night off Greenhithe, intending to make a bold start in the morning. Lying a little below us we saw the *Will Everard*, also loaded, and on the way ashore we met one of her crew on the causeway.

'Where are you for?' asked the lad from the *Will*, partly out of professional interest and partly because he and Ken both had designs on the same girl in Yarmouth.

'A.B.C. wharf.'

'So are we. Better pull your socks up tomorrow.'

And pull our socks up we did.

It was not much of a day for sailing but we both mustered in good heart and no sooner were anchors up than they were quickly fished on the bow and boltsprits lowered down to accommodate two jibs apiece. Running down the river the barges kept close together, sometimes one getting a lucky puff and sometimes the other.

Clear of Southend the water was smooth and we drew ahead a little, having the advantage of having cleaned her bottom of weeds and barnacles recently while we had been unloading at Colchester.

As night fell we were off the Whitaker Beacon at the entrance to the River Crouch. Ahead we could see a bunch of other barges at anchor, waiting for the flood tide to give them enough water to cross the Spitway — a shallow low-way off Clacton between the Buxey and Gunfleet Sands.

The *Will* and the *Greenhithe* just saved the last of the ebb to the vicinity of the Spitway buoy and there we had to anchor. The flood had run about three hours when there came a smart breeze from the north-west. The moon was not yet up and we got our anchor as quickly and quietly as we could, got the canvas on her and kept the riding light up in the hope that the crew of the *Will* would think we were still brought up. This ruse gave us a useful start on the other barge because we heard the master of the *Will* shout (somewhat angrily) to his crew 'Heave that bloody anchor up. They're under way with a riding light up.'

But we were past them by then and stretching away across the Spitway into the Wallet Channel. She was after us like a bloodhound on the trail and with every stitch set we sailed right through the fleet of other barges, who were commencing to cross the Spitway, as though they were brought up.

The wind freshened. The *Will* gained on us and hauled out to windward. We held her off until we reached the Naze and then, as we opened out Dovercourt Bay and began to stagger with the extra weight of wind, the *Will* came by us. It was moonlight by then and I could see that she was travelling like a thoroughbred under conditions which suited her admirably. Soon our big jib topsail had to come in, so much water were we shipping to leeward. But our bigger rival could bear all her canvas and in the few miles across the Stone Banks to Hollesley Bay she must have gained nearly two miles.

At crack of day the wind fell light again and we saw the *Will* close in under Aldeburgh while we were about two miles astern and a mile or so further offshore. Fitful airs came from all directions and we made up the distance we had lost in the night, drawing level but a long way to leeward. Then both barges were becalmed for a time and being further out in the ebb stream I daresay we drifted a bit faster to the northward than the other barge.

When the breeze came the luck was all ours. It was east. Instead of being a mile to leeward we were a mile to windward of her and moreover were the first to feel the wind. Away we went with the sheets slacked off while astern the *Will* had to claw off the land to get a safer offing before being free enough to chase us.

But she could not catch the *Greenhithe* then. As we approached Yarmouth pierheads we saw the tug coming out to meet us. I signalled her to keep clear while we sailed right into the harbour and up against the ebb to the A.B.C. wharf.

The *Will* seemed to have lost heart and was struggling along some four of five miles astern. The tug went out to fetch her in while we got ready to discharge.

We won that day — but the luck had been with us. Her day was to come.

Pierheads in Bad Weather

IN the hurly burly life of coasting under canvas it was hardly noticeable for a time that our companions in sail were gradually getting fewer and fewer. But a few years after the war had ended there came a rather rapid decline in the red sailed fleets that used to set out from London for the East Coast ports and we could do a round trip from London to Yarmouth, the Humber and back to London without seeing a single barge under sail.

Sometimes when lying in the docks in London in company with other barges I would ask for news of vessels which seemed to have slipped out of existence.

'Where's the old so-and-so? Haven't seen her about lately.'

'Oh, she's gone to have her engine put in' — or — 'she's been sold for a yacht' — or — 'she's being turned into a houseboat' — or, worse still — 'she's being broken up.'

It seemed incredible to think that just before the war broke out I had been among fifty-one barges getting under way together from Sea Reach, outward bound after a spell of easterly weather. The river mouth was a mass of bellying canvas, the barges almost aboard of one another and not room for a steamboat to get past them. There was some smart seamanship to be seen on days like that and a sailorman who did not know his job could bring accident and disaster to himself and several others by a false manoeuvre or bad judgement.

But all that was done. We became lonelier and lonelier. People began to marvel at us being able to get from place to place in reasonable time without the assistance of an engine and that in itself was an indication that a sailing barge was well on the way to becoming a curio in the new era of machine-driven ships.

Month by month, year by year, little odd incidents began to impress upon me that the days of sail were nearly over at last. I remember once when we were heaving the *Greenhithe* into the dock at King's Lynn, holding up a motor ship for a few minutes while we did so, to the great annoyance of her skipper and pilot. Some lads on the deck of a training ship nearby were watching, some with pity and some with derision, and I heard one of them remark that he believed we had come from London without an engine.

'Then how did she get here?' asked his companion. 'Strewth! I wouldn't go to sea in that.'

These were British boys being trained as seamen. As we sprung the barge ahead round the dockhead knuckle with a line on the leeboard crab winch I realised, judging by their attitude of wonder and ridicule, that to these bright lads of the new generation such sailormen as we might just as well belong to the Stone Age.

There were still a fair number of river barges, mostly in the cement and ballast work, but, like us big 'uns, their days were numbered as new motor craft came to be built. In the small barges the crews could not earn a decent living in face of competition from fast power craft and the coasting barges had to be thankful for any cargo they could get — and then deliver it as quickly as possible so as not to show up too badly against the motors. In fact there was more pressing and cracking on and sleepless nights in this last struggle for survival than there had been in the flourishing days of coasting sail.

Young Ken left after twelve months to join his father aboard a new floating oil refinery. There was good pay for him there and the prospect of steady advancement. He liked the barges and was none too eager to go but he realised, being a young man, that he had better start carving out his career in a job that was going to lead to something.

For his last freight we loaded raw sugar in Ipswich Dock, and when the news got round among the barging fraternity that the mate of the *Greenhithe* was leaving young Hazelton (who had been mate with me for three months while waiting to take the *Saltcote Bell*) jumped aboard and asked for his old job back. He had had enough of the *Saltcote Belle* when she fell short of work and seemed very pleased to get back to the *Greenhithe*.

He was a very different type from Ken Fry but a fine seaman all the same. He had been aboard barges from schoolboy days and I can only say that he deserved the somewhat hackneyed phrase of being 'quietly efficient'.

With Hazelton as mate and his young friend Jim Godfrey, also of Ipswich, as third hand, I had as good a crew as any barge skipper could wish for. Hazelton was sensible, workmanlike and experienced while Godfrey (unlike many third hands in barges) was clean, obedient and a good cook.

We were a happy ship. They relied on me and I knew that I could rely on them.

It was while they were my crew that we once made a spectacular entry into Lowestoft harbour in a gale of wind on a Sunday and made a lot of people late for church. We had flour in for the wharf in the Inner Harbour and had made a fast night passage from London in rough weather. Between the North-east Gunfleet and Southwold so many seas had peeled the full length of her deck that she was as clean as a new pin. The ship was, but the crew were not. We had had no time for such luxuries as washing and shaving and in any case we were too anxious to get into harbour to worry about what we looked like. It took two of us to steer and the gallant Jim, wet and weary, emerged periodically with mugs of steaming tea or cocoa and sandwiches which can only be described as hefty, each one being a meal in itself. In between times he saw to the navigation lights at night, kept an eye on the lashings and wedges, tended the leeboard winches when required and carried out the many duties which the mate did not have time to do when helping me at the wheel.

Approaching the South Barnard buoy, which was rearing up and down like a kid's Jack-in-the-box, the wind backed to the south-east and it was obvious that the gale was likely to become worse. But I had a plan in mind and I knew of a low way across the Barnard shoals into Pakefield Road, which runs close under the cliffs to the south of Lowestoft. Once in this in-shore channel we could run close to Lowestoft pierheads and see if conditions were fit to take the harbour. If not we should have to run on through Yarmouth Roads and probably round the Cockle to find shelter off the sandy beaches along by Winterton and Haisborough.

The Barnard shoal looked white and wicked. The seas were steep and curly, too much like the breakers on a sandy beach to feel comfortable, even though I was confident that there was enough water for us. Young Jim, being a better third hand than most, was trusted with the lead because I wanted the mate to help me at the wheel. He was a good helmsman and when I needed to step clear of the wheelhouse to judge my bearings he struggled manfully and kept her from gybing or broaching-to.

Jim called three fathoms, then three again, then two and a half, not quite two and a half (I stopped breathing for a bit when he said this), then two and a half again, thank God), three, three and a half. All was well. We were in Pakefield Road.

We eased our mainsheet a little and sped along by the beaches towards the stone walls of Lowestoft harbour. The seas were thundering on the pierheads, sending up clouds of spray and presenting to us weary mariners a fearsome aspect. But we were looking at the worst side, the windward side, of the harbour entrance, and with a free wind such as we had I knew that she ought to go in. She was nicely loaded, being not too deep and a bit by the stern, and was travelling at such a rate that she would batter her way through the broken water in the opening.

Hazelton looked at me inquiringly. He was a bit anxious — and he had reason to be by the look of the spray flying over the south pier. I told him that we would take the harbour.

'Down jib and up bobstay as soon as she's inside, and get your anchor off the bow.'

I had the pair of them pull in the mainsheet as far as they could, up to their backsides in water at times, and then heave the weather vang in on the crab winch. With everything trimmed ready for either a luff or a bear up, I ran her off shore a little and then headed in for the entrance.

It was not so bad as it had looked. She careered through the confused and broken water in the entrance like a bronco and as we gained the welcome shelter of the harbour walls I saw two men on one of the inner piers vigorously beckoning to us to keep coming.

'They're ready for you with the bridge,' they yelled.

This was indeed a great slice of luck. Instead of performing intricate manoeuvres within the confines of the outer harbour in order to get the sail off her and probably let go the anchor, we could now go surging up through the cutting right into our berth. The older men on the swing bridge, which carries the roadway through the town, had in days gone by been accustomed to making a quick swing if they saw a sailing smack taking the harbour in rough weather and unable to check her way. There used to be a big fleet of splendid ketches belonging to Lowestoft and my forbears had owned and sailed in them. I had sailed to South

America in one of them and although she was only fifty-seven feet long I had kept my feet drier than I did in the old *Greenhithe*.

Heeling over with the weight of wind in her topsail, the barge glided swiftly up the narrow cutting, through the bridgehole and into the Inner Harbour. We were so busy with our own affairs that it was only then that I noticed we were being watched by a great crowd of people. Apparently we had virtually split the population of Lowestoft into two sections, marooned on each side of the opened bridge.

It transpired that when the harbour master saw that we were safely within the outer walls he had stopped all traffic and got the bridge open in good time. There everyone was compelled to stop and watch our little struggle, whether they were interested or not and I have to confess to a little touch of conceit as we went sailing up between them and through the centre of the town.

Things had to happen quickly while this was being done. I rapped out orders to the mate and third hand and they jumped to it like a couple of heroes. It is on occasions like this when an inefficient crew can bungle the whole affair and cause the ship, themselves and the master's reputation a deal of damage.

Down jib, up bobstay, anchor off the bow, brail up your mainsail, down foresail, down topsail, clew in your topsail sheet, lower the boat in the water, swing your davits in, fenders ready to go alongside. I will hand it to Hazelton that I have never seen a mate fly round a barge's deck as fast as he did during the few minutes he had to do all these things. But, with Jim's help, he accomplished it.

I learned afterwards that when the crew were recognised ashore that evening there was more than one pot of ale stood up for them — 'for the lads in that barge what took the harbour this morning'.

They deserved it, too, for they had been a credit to the old *Greenhithe* that day.

Beaten after 180 miles

———————— ❀ ————————

WE had just unloaded in Colchester a cargo of cement from London River and had orders to proceed to Keadby to load coal back to Colchester Gas Works. There was a fickle south-west wind and fine weather and on the morning tide we ambled down between the fields in anticipation of a leisurely passage in settled weather. It was July.

The *Greenhithe's* bottom was getting a bit weedy but in the soft mud berth where we had been unloading it had not been possible to scrub her. But being bound back to a hard bottom berth I thought that the cleaning off was a matter which could wait for a week or so without slowing her up too much.

But when we passed the Naze and I spotted the topsail of the *Will Everard* coming out of Harwich harbour I thought 'That's torn it. She's caught us with a dirty bottom.'

I knew that the *Will* must be bound to Keadby as well for the wind was 'down along' and the tide had just started to ebb.

'Tumble up there,' I called to the crew, who were stowing away some gear below. 'Fetch up that ballooner. Here comes the *Will Everard.*'

Unfortunately that ballooner, a huge light foresail, was made for the *Cambria* and not the *Greenhithe* and was miles too big to set properly. Normally we only used it in very calm weather to keep way on the barge in light airs.

By the time we had cut across the Stone Banks the *Will* was out of the harbour and coming after us with her bowsprit down and two jibs set. It was soon obvious that she was steadily overhauling us.

I racked my brains as I steered for some scheme to outwit her but found none. She was a bigger, faster, handier and more weatherly ship and we always needed some measure of advantage to beat her on a clear sea run — a clean bottom, a favourable shift of wind, a cut across the shallows or something to go wrong aboard the *Will*.

We held her off down through Hollesley Bay and round Orfordness, but off Aldeburgh she was up on our quarter and, hanging there for a while as the breeze became paltry, forged ahead as the wind grew stronger. By nightfall she was about a mile in front of us.

We saw no stern light shine from the *Will Everard* that night. Her crew were not going to give us a mark to steer after. So through the darkness we ploughed along, keeping a sharp lookout, trimming sheets and leeboards, slacking a bit here, hauling a bit there, trying to get the best out of the old *Greenhithe* without any hope or thought of sleep.

Three pairs of bleary eyes searched the sea at the first break in the gloom. Hazelton went up the rigging a little way and then came aft.

'I think I can see her; not so very far ahead.'

But she was far enough to take a lot of catching.

As dawn spread we saw her plainly, some two miles north of us, making best use of what had become a fair wind. She had a balloon foresail boomed out as a spinnaker and her big staysail squared off above it. Alas! We had no spinnaker boom and could only push our ballooner out on the end of a boathook.

We never caught her again, though once when the wind drew ahead and our rival made a short board off Cromer we picked up a lot of lost ground. When the *Greenhithe* ran into the Humber we could see the *Will* going up by

Killingholme. That night — the tide done — we had to anchor west of Reed Island and the *Will* was some five or six miles ahead in the River Trent. Next day we dropped alongside her at the Keadby coal wharf, beaten but not disgraced.

Both barges were loaded quickly and the tug *Waterman* came to take the pair of us down to Hull Roads. As she cast us off bowsprits were lowered and all sails set, each barge carrying mainsail, topsail, foresail, two jibs and mizzen. Tack and tack we went down round the Skitter Sand. We had towed astern of the *Will* so she had a little lead of us but we were close aboard of her off Killingholme and she had to luff hard to keep us from getting to windward of her. There was a chance that while in smooth water we might gain a little advantage so I had to employ an old racing ruse to get through her lee. There was no hope of my barge out-luffing her.

'She'll luff again — sure to' I told the mate and third hand. 'When she does stand by the mainsheet and vang fall and slack everything well off as I up helm.'

The *Will* luffed again and even thought to fox me with the age-old bluff of having the hands run to the jib sheets as though she was coming about across our head. This gave us our chance. Up went our helm and the mate and third hand let the sheet and vang run well off as the *Greenhithe* bore away. As the wind was brought abeam she quickly gathered speed to leeward as the *Will* lost way with her headsails all ashake. As the big barge lost way we gained it. The *Greenhithe* went careering under the *Will's* stern and before the latter bore up and filled away again we got our sheet and vang in and the barge on the wind again. With the extra speed she had gained the *Greenhithe* shot out of the big barge's lee and danced off down the Humber ahead of her.

This little triumph was short lived. As we stood out of the Humber round Donna Nook the wind was about south-south-west and this meant a passage across to Cromer on a

99

tight sheet. And on a tight sheet the *Greenhithe* hadn't a
hope of holding the *Will Everard*. Quickly she worked out
to windward of us and all I could do was keep the *Greenhithe*
a point free and let her go across the Inner Dowsing Shoal
and up by the Race Bank, while the *Will* hauled inshore
into less broken water. She looked a long way away from us
but we travelled the shorter distance and when our courses
converged on Cromer the *Will* was only about a couple of
miles in the lead. She gained a little more by the time
darkness closed on us.

It was a fine night with the wind tending to wester and
before dawn I turned in and left Hazelton to do the best
he could with her from the Cockle up through Caister and
Yarmouth Roads.

When he called me it was daylight, he had worked her
up along the shore against the ebb and there was the *Will*
only a few hundred yards ahead and slightly to leeward. By
the time the flood tide started the barges were ramping up
through Lowestoft North Road, the distance between them
being only about a quarter of a mile; and I daresay they
made a fine sight for any early riser on the land. It was
blowing a fresh wind by then — due west — and once more
I saw a chance to put the *Greenhithe* in the lead. Off the
Inner Shoal the *Will*, shy of the broken water, went off to
leeward a little and I could see her mate casting the lead.
But here I was in waters that my family had fished and sailed
for generations and it is one of those places where broken
swell is not always a sign of the shallowest water. So with
one eye of Lowestoft Church spire and the other on the
compass I steered through the white froth, skated the outer
edge of the Inner Shoal with the leeboard just clear of the
bottom, and came out over the Barnard Sand with the *Will*
trailing astern. My crew were jubilant, but once more their
joy was short lived.

A moderate squall came off the land and for a few
moments out barge was overcanvassed. We should have

Coal from the North

taken in the staysail which was set above the bowsprit jib and put a heavy strain on the topmast.

I saw the topmast nod forward and the mate quickly put a preventer tackle on the running backstay. No one was going to suggest taking in sail now that at last we were ahead again. But the topmast lurched forward again. The weather cross-tree had buckled and to the accompaniment of some of the worst language I have ever heard aboard a barge the staysail had to come down. But Hazelton's blood was up and without a word from me he dashed down the forecastle and emerged with a coil of cargo wire. Up aloft he clambered like a cat — out on to the buckled cross-tree without a sign of fear or hesitation. The end of this wire he shackled to the outer part of the cross-tree and then slid down to the deck on a backstay and a much greater speed than could be called either safe or comfortable. Within a matter of seconds he and the third hand had got the wire aft and on to the barrel of the leeboard winch. Together they hove the bent cross-tree back far enough to set the staysail again.

It was a brilliant piece of initiative, seamanship and daring and worthy of the best traditions which had been built up in these coasting barges. I think it was the smartest five minutes' work I have seen the mate of a barge accomplish.

But in spite of this gallant effort I knew that the *Will* would catch us if the wind did not veer so that we could keep our sheets slacked off after passing Ordfordness. And although we kept ahead of her and were first to pass the lighthouse, the dead peg to windward from there gave the powerful *Will* every advantage. She took it, too. While the *Greenhithe*, sagging away to leeward, close hauled as she could be, fetched the Rough buoy, the *Will* slipped to windward and with one short board fetched the Cork Lightship. So she was ahead once more. As the ebb came away we both struggled on a few more tacks, loth to bring up. When the *Will* was up past the Naze and the *Greenhithe* in Dovercourt Bay, both barges had to anchor for the rest of the ebb.

Neither crew lost any time heaving anchors up and getting the canvas set as the evening flood came but in turning up the Wallet Channel past Clacton and in to the Colne the *Will* held her lead and anchored off Brightlingsea as my barge was coming by the Inner Bench Head. We watched her riding light go up and although my crew were a bit despondent at being beaten they had worked like Trojans and done well to hold a bigger and better barge to a matter of a couple of miles after a hundred and eighty miles passage.

This was the last sail we ever had against the *Will* because her skipper was keen on having an engine installed. She went on the shipyard to emerge some months later as a well powered auxiliary.

I have described this impromptu race in some detail because I believe it is probably the last occasion on which two commercial sailing vessels have vied with each other at sea in the course of every day trading.

Rough Run back and a Long Trick

WITH the eclipse of the *Will Everard* from the ranks of sailing barges we in the *Greenhithe* ploughed a truly lonely furrow. We continued to trade to the estuary ports — Yarmouth, Norwich, and up with coal from Keadby to Harwich and Colchester — but there were times when we did not see a sail for weeks; and ashore in the old haunts where bargemen used to gather we found only a few steamboatmen and wharfside workers.

In the autumn we went on the yard for our annual survey and 'do-up' and while here I lost Hazelton. Worse still, Jim Godfrey was 'shanghaied' to do his National Service; thus, like young Ken Fry, being forced to become a soldier at a time when he showed the makings of a good sailorman. I was very sorry to see them go.

Eventually I was joined by a young man named Joe Bowles who had been mate of the *Felix* and third hand of the *Will Everard*. A dark, tough lad, he looked like a miniature Jack Dempsey and was much admired by the girls in every port. In fact Joe had such an attractive personality (to them) that they used to row out in boats to greet him as soon as the barge's anchor was down. Son of a famous fishing skipper who had once won the Prunier

Trophy for the best herring catch of the season off the East Anglian coast, Joe proved to be a good worker and a faithful mate. His great drawback was that in spite of several years at sea he was prone to a distressing sickness in bad weather. This curse he seemed never able to throw off and every time we had a bad blow Joe was almost out of commission. This was a serious disadvantage to me and meant that on one occasion I had to do an eighteen hour trick at the wheel.

We loaded bulk linseed in Colchester for Hull. Joe worked like a Trojan trimming the barge with this seed, which runs and slithers more than any other type of bulk cargo and if badly trimmed would easily shift at sea.

Aboard at the time was another ex-fishing boat lad as third hand but being used to power winches I could see he did not relish the hand hauling and heaving to be done aboard a sailing barge.

We sailed in fine weather — it was late February — and for extra company we had a hardy working passenger named Howard Smith (by profession a Patent Office Examiner) who had done a lot of yacht sailing in heavy boats and turned to with a will when there was any lugging and grunting to be done. I was glad of his companionship. Soon I was to be glad of his help. He was keen to make a passage to the Humber under sail as it looked as though the *Greenhithe* was likely to be the last sailing vessel to ply the waters of this arduous trade. He had obtained special leave from his office.

'I've read a lot about east coast sailing colliers,' he said, 'and I have never yet sailed into the Humber.'

So he made himself comfortable on the cabin locker, prepared to get a glimpse of what the life was really like. Of course, with a little luck and fair winds the Humber trade can be quite profitable to a sailing barge: but without luck and with gales and headwinds it can be a wearisome and exhausting business. Sometimes day after day, night after night, with no hope of rest or sleep or proper food, the bargeman feels that it is indeed a rough way to earn a living.

Hythe Quay, where we loaded, has a pleasant, old world touch about it and when a fleet of sailing barges used to be moored alongside it the place was worth a moment's pause even if you were in a hurry. Yet for all its sleepy look there was nothing sleepy about the work that went on there. It is the only port I have been in where the Harbour Master stands ready to receive every ship or barge, big or small, that comes in, day or night, week day or Sunday. It is one of the few places where the *Greenhithe* could discharge 170 tons of coal in four hours with only a single, small crane. It is one of the few places where men set about their work 'to get the job done' without pulling out a book of union rules every five minutes and complaining about the difficulties. It is one of the few ports where the broker's office is on the quay and not hidden away in some deep recess of the city as in so many places. Also, by stepping across the road from the quay one can obtain a really good pint of beer. And, what's more, Hythe is only an hour's bus ride from my cottage at Pin Mill. These last two points are very important advantages.

We loaded our cargo by means of a wooden shute, down which the sacks of linseed were emptied. The men wheeled them out of the warehouse on hand trucks and across a raised platform which spanned the road. The shute led from the end of this construction down into the barge's hold.

Before loading started the mate swept the hold clean and conscientiously removed every trace of coal dust. He was somewhat wrath when a Ministry of Food official arrived, peeped down the hatchway and said: 'Captain, I want that hold swept up before you start to load.'

This official, down from London, was there to supervise the loading of the cargo and I suspect that as he had not very much to do but watch us work he wished to make his presence felt.

When I passed his remark on to the mate he nearly exploded.

'If he can get that blank blank hold any cleaner than that he can blank blank well try and he can stick this blank broom — '. I've forgotten all he said but you know what barge mates are when they get upset. I sympathetically reasoned with him and pointed out that it would be as well not to aggravate the gentleman from the Ministry as work for sailing barges at that time was not too plentiful and the Ministry were giving us fairly regular cargoes. So we made a great bustle and show with large brooms, getting out of his sight under the deck and banging the sides of the barge loudly with the broom handles.

Satisfied that he had made his presence felt, he went off to lunch. So did we. When he came back I took him to the hatchway and pointed down the hold.

'There,' I said in the manner of a man who is proud of his work, 'what do you think of that for a clean hold?'

'Ah, that's better,' he said; which proved that his lunch must have done him a power of good considering that we had not done anything else to the hold. Joe had previously swept it clean enough to load anything and a second sweeping would have been a waste of time and effort. But there, what's the good of being an official without being officious.

By the time the after end of the hold was three parts full the mate and third hand jumped down, armed with shovels, and trimmed the linseed under the decks, pushing it in every hole and corner as tight as possible so that it would not run and shift in a seaway. And when the work became tiring the thought of 'more tons more dollars' kept the shovels swinging doggedly until we sweated a mixture of dust, beer and linseed oil.

We were two days loading and succeeded in cramming $167\frac{1}{2}$ tons in to her. The *Greenhithe* had a fine big hold but linseed takes up a lot of room per ton. As soon as the loading was finished we covered up and battened down ready for sea. As the tide flowed buckets and scrubbers were got to work so that we were trim and clean by the time the grocer arrived with the rations.

When all these preparations were completed it was nearly dark. Off I went, home to Pin Mill, leaving the crew to make a last gallant attempt to drink all the beer in Colchester and take what pleasure they might in the several feminine friendships as they seemed able to strike up at very short notice.

The next day, at two o'clock in the afternoon, the little harbour launch came to help us down through the narrows. The wind was southerly, and when the motor boat cast us off by Alresford Creek we set the mainsail, topsail and foresail and proceeded down the river in short tacks until below Brightlingsea. There the barge's boat was hove up in the davits and securely lashed. The mate fished the anchor on the bow, lowered the bowsprit and set a medium sized jib. The third hand lit the sidelights and stern light, and away we went into the gathering gloom, to and fro on a tight sheet until we reached the bar buoy. One more tack to clear the Eagle Sand and we slacked away our canvas for a night's run, hoping to be in Yarmouth Roads by daylight. The wind was fresh and continued for the most time southerly, so with the ebb tide under us we sloshed along past Clacton and down the Wallet Channel to the Naze. A little homesick peep at the lights of Harwich (so near home and yet so far!) and off across the shallow uneven banks to the Cork Lightship. From there we could see the steady stream of motor and steam coasters coming out of the Barrow Deeps and heading northwards round Orfordness, many of them no doubt ships of our own company.

The third hand turned in after supper, for when all was well he had the privilege of sleeping all night. He was the youngest and got the lowest wages; moreover I have never believed in keeping young lads on deck for long hours at night unless making harbour or caught in bad weather. If they are going to be sailormen they will know enough of long hours and sleepless nights when they grow older. But they have to grow first.

The mate also had a spell on his back, taking the wheel after we were clear of the Whiting Sand and safely round Orfordness. With the great light flashing on our sails and making the barge look like something out of a ghost story, I sipped a welcome cup of cocoa and then rolled into my bunk all standing save my boots. Joe knew this bit of coast pretty well and there were no off-lying dangers to speak of, so I dozed off peacefully to the pleasant sound of water gurgling past the starboard quarter.

I awoke three hours later. It was crack of day and I slipped up the companion ladder in my socks. Joe stood at the wheel in the half light, looking like a sentinel, his eyes alternating between the compass and the little flag at the topmast head.

'How goes?' I asked.

'Just passed the East Barnard. Ebb's still running hard.'

Lowestoft lights looked a bit hard and clear and the first sign of sunrise was a great red glow out to seaward. I pulled on a thick jersey and took the wheel from the mate.

'Shove the kettle on and call the boy.'

Joe did as he was bid and the sleepy lad was rousted out of his heavenly dreams. By the time the great mugs of tea had been swilled down and breakfast cooked the sun had climbed into an overcast sky and taken on a greasy, unhealthy look which coasting men associate with bad weather.

There was a longish swell rolling shorewards through the Stanford Channel and by the time we were off Goreleston the wind had backed to the south-east and there was enough breaking water to come tumbling over the rail by the mainhorse and sweep forward along the decks as far as the mastcase. It was going to blow all right, but south-east is a fair wind for the Humber.

Our Hardy Passenger helped the lads tighten up the hatchway lashings, tap the wedges and make sure that everything was snug and fast. I did not like the look of things but while the wind was south-seat there was no going back. I used to reassure myself on coastal runs in threatening weather that a barge will generally go one way or the other — back to where she came from or on to her destination — provided vital decisions were made soon enough.

There was quite a sea running at the Cockle and when we were well round Winterton Ness the wind was more easterly and blowing hard. The mizzen was stowed and shortly after the head of the topsail was run down, leaving the barge under full mainsail and sheet of the topsail, foresail and bowsprit jib. With this rig she was reasonably handy in bad weather and under it had come through many a nasty gale since the day I took charge of her some ten years before.

But although the barge was all right the crew — alas — were not. Grievously vomiting and groaning the pair of them lay down in the forecastle and only our Hardy Passenger remained on deck to lend me a hand.

As we opened out Cromer pier and could see the town, a great black cloud appeared in the sky to the north-east. We were then charging along with the wind about east-south-east but as we approached this black barrier across the sky the slacked off mainsail gave a violent kick and we ran slap into a vicious north-easterly squall. I bellowed for the hands to come up on deck and like two bilious ghosts they laboured at the mainsheet and weather vang to trim the barge on the wind. This done, with the help of the lee-board winch barrel, we managed to get the vessel heading slightly off shore but a heavy sea soon built up and started to break across the hatches.

I knew that this was no temporary squall but the fore-runner of a north-east gale. It is a wicked wind on this part of the coast and although it is possible to lay a course for the Humber the beam seas may drive a barge so far to leeward that she becomes embayed and likely to drive on one of the numerous shoals close in shore between Blakeney and Burnham Flats. And if the skipper leaves it too late before deciding to turn back the barge may not be able to weather Cromer again and finish up as did the poor old *Hibernia* (*Cambria's* sister ship), a beautiful barge built by Mr Fred Everard, which had laid her bones on the beach there for lack of an offing in a wild north-easter.

So I decided to run back. The Hardy Passenger and I got her round on to the port tack and once more the sick and weary emerged to brail up three cloths of the mainsail.

The ebb was away and a steep white-smeared sea made steering a battle of brute strength. I had persuaded the shipyard not long before to let me have a larger size wheel and I was thankful on this occasion for the extra leverage it afforded. After some hours of this Joe staggered aft and gallantly tried to help; but he was not fit to steer and after vomiting all over the wheelhouse so that I could not get a proper foothold he retired once more and I relied on our Hardy Passenger. Prejudiced against passengers by tradition, I was thankful he was there. He managed to produce a cup of cocoa and acted as lee helmsman as I began to tire.

When we arrived back at the Cockle and opened up Caister Road I could see big steamships heaving and plunging in a wicked sea and it was obvious that we were not to find respite in any of the roadsteads off Yarmouth. So on we rolled and lurched. Sometimes I had to climb up the lee spokes of the wheel like a ladder to get the old cow to bear up when heavy seas chucked her weather quarter up in the air and threatened to broach her to.

Hour after hour went by and, hardly realising the passage of time, it came as quite a shock to notice that night was closing in again and the lights were up on shore. By this time we were out of the white capped Stanford Channel off Lowestoft and pitching along past Southwold, some two miles off shore. Aldeburgh, Ordfordness light — and then (Thank God) the seas began to die down. In Hollesley Bay the Hardy Passenger solved the mysteries of the brail

winch and let up the pawl so that I could set a full mainsail
again. The weather, even here with a bit of a lee under the
shingle bank, was not fit for us to anchor so on we rolled
towards the lights of Felixstowe.

The mate and third hand had by this time recovered
sufficiently to appear on deck again as ordinary humans
bearing some slight resemblance to British seamen. The
topsail was set and we hauled our wind round the Beach
End buoy into the peace and quietness of Harwich harbour.

Silently in the dark the *Greenhithe* glided by the Guard
and round into the River Stour, past the rows of mooring
buoys to an anchoring berth off Shotley pier. Sails were
stowed and the noise of the mate chucking the chain over
the windlass was the only thing that disturbed the stillness
of a harbour night.

Above us I could see the clouds still bustling across the
sky and I knew that away off Cromer it was probably
blowing just as hard as when we turned back.

I was too weary to help the crew with the sails or leeboards. I felt I had done my bit that day. It was midnight —
and I had had that wheel in my hands for eighteen hours
without relief or a bite to eat — only the cup of cocoa that
the Hardy Passenger had made off the Cockle. My arms
and shoulders ached, my legs and feet felt leaden and
swollen. I went below and subsided into my bunk. We had
sailed from Colchester for the Humber — been to Cromer
and arrived in Harwich.

After two days the north-east wind fined away almost to a
calm and then gave way to a moderate south-west breeze.
The Hardy Passenger's leave was up and, his ambition to
sail to the Humber still unsatisfied, he had to bid us farewell
and return to London.

With fresh stores and fresh energy we sailed away from
Shotley and in smooth water and fine weather we made an
easy passage north, bringing up in Hull Roads exactly
twenty-four hours after weighing anchor at Shotley.

We unloaded our linseed in the dock there and then got orders to load coal at Keadby for Colchester. We sailed out of the dock, to the consternation of the dockmaster (they are not used to a barge's ways there) and reached away up the river to the Trent, where we had to contend with a persistent headwind which kept us tacking patiently between the reeds but draining up to windward rapidly owing to the swiftness of the tidal stream.

There was the usual homely welcome at Keadby. Folk there know you by your Christian name, help you moor up, ask after old friends and inquire the whereabouts of other sailormen. However much coasting men may curse the Trent coal cargoes I have never heard any of them regret the brief sojourn among the Keadby people.

We loaded our coal for Colchester Gas Works and after a splendid start from the Humber, running at a steady eight and a half knots from off Mablethorpe to Blakeney Overfalls, the wind backed from west-south-west to south and started to pipe. By the time we were off Sheringham we had run into a full gale and I had the topsail clewed in and stowed, jib hauled down and securely lashed on the bowsprit and the mizzen brailed and gasketed.

For awhile she plunged along under foresail and full mainsail while we closed the land on the ebb, by which time it was pitch dark. Under the lee of the cliffs I hove her to on the starboard tack. It was a bad gale and a black, fierce night. She rode well, shipping a few seas when caught on the wrong roll but generally behaving almost as manfully as a smack. Her bold head and high ends were certainly a help to her under those conditions.

Of course, I could have run her back to the Humber in reasonable safety and comfort but was loth to give up so many vital miles so hard to gain on this particular stretch of coast. The wind was sure to veer in time. Twice big steamships came to us with searchlights thinking we were in trouble; and probably we looked a sorry picture in their eyes, with spray going right over us and water continually swirling round the decks. A small motor coaster rounded to near us and lay there for a while, no doubt anxious about us, but it was hopeless to try and hear a hail, even down-wind. As the wind started to veer with heavy showers of rain, the little coaster went on her way. I never did find out her name.

Shortly after daylight the wind came well off from the south-west and we let draw the foresail and started to make some progress past Cromer towards Haisborough, although the gale was still howling like the devil. However, I felt quite content and hoped that as it blew out it would die from the north-west and give us a fair slant. But it was not long before I was to get a nasty shock.

The third hand came up out of the forecastle twice as fast as he generally moved and came running aft with a face like the end of time.

'There's a lot of water on the forecastle floor.'

This round trip seemed doomed to misfortune. We were leaking. Must have sprung some rivets in the gale.

I put the mate at the wheel and went forward. With the boy's help I prised up a portion of the forecastle flooring and underneath was some two feet of water, washing up menacingly on the lee side. For a while I was a bit puzzled as to how to set about finding the leak without having to run the barge on the beach, which I did not want to do if it could possibly be avoided. Then I noticed a slight disturbance in the swaying water and made a hopeful guess that this was where the water was coming in. I plunged my arm down and felt about on the steel plate of her bottom just forward of the watertight bulkhead which separated the forecastle from the hold. I could not find the hole. I seized the galley poker and used that to reach further down.

Suddenly the poker went down and a fountain of water squirted up. I had found the hole alright! The poker had gone right down through her bottom. The leak proved later to be a tiny thin patch in an otherwise perfectly sound plate.

Frantically I grabbed a towel and some rags and reached down a full arm's length in the water and bunged them hard in the hole. The boy got the forward pump working and I dashed off aft to fetch a big wooden fid, four feet long, which I kept for splicing tow ropes. This I hammered into the leak, filling in the broken edges of the hole with firewood chips. This checked the water and slowly the pump began to gain. Three hours later we had pumped all the water out and I was able to effect a better stoppage though still using my fid as the main plug.

Soon the gale subsided to a fresh wind from the west and we got the jib on her again and rattled up through Yarmouth Roads at about seven knots, the wind freeing out all the time. Next day we sailed into the River Colne, having had to pump out forward every two hours but glad to be in calm and safety once more.

In response to a phone call, shipwrights from Greenhithe yard came down to Colchester by lorry, repaired the leak by putting in a 'cement box' and soon we were fit to go to sea again.

A few more freights, without undue excitement, and we had to go on the slipway for our general load line survey. This is a very strict inspection by a Ministry official. There was a lot to be done and labour was short. All the replating necessary would take a long time. Once more I was offered command of a motor ship — once more I refused.

I knew that without sails and a kicking wheel I might as well go ashore. I was getting too old to change my ways and become a proper captain in a smart hat and uniform. So go ashore I did, picking up a land job and doing a bit of in-shore trawl fishing with my old sailing smack *Stormy Petrel*. But she had no power like the other smacks and could not catch trains and markets: so there was not much profit in that. But fortunately our little hamlet of Pin Mill, on the south bank of the lovely Orwell, is a sailorman's village and the native soil of half the skippers whoever sailed out of Ipswich and Harwich; and of a good many who migrated to the Medway.

Living ashore at Pin Mill was not like abandoning salt water altogether. Most people did a bit of fishing, talked about barges and sailed in yachts. In our little row of cottages, where the gardens have all tasted the Orwell's highest tides, there lived bargemen, fishermen and even a deep sea diver who started his career as a lad in the Ipswich spritties. So the talk in the two inns, the Butt and Oyster and the Riga, always had a strong flavour of salt water.

In my spare time I set about finishing this book and this might well have been the end of the manuscript but for a telephone call from Everards at Greenhithe, followed by a letter from one of the 'guv'nors.'

Would I go back and take the *Cambria*? Her old skipper had fallen ill and retired. I was half afraid to tell my wife but I suppose she watched me pacing up and down the front room, looking at the pictures of ships and barges which hung round the walls. She knew, better than I did, that a shore job to me was only a stepping stone to the grave.

'Why don't you go back? You'll never be happy or well without a wheel in your hand.'

Not many men, certainly not many sailors, have a wife who would say that! So to Greenhithe I went, kitbag on back, and joined the handsome old *Cambria*.

She was (perhaps I should say she *is*) a sturdy wooden barge, ninety-one feet long, and bears the distinction of being the last coaster left under sail in Great Britain. She was laid down by the late Mr Fred Everard, who started the present day company, and built under the supervision of his son Mr William Everard. His elder brother, Mr Fred, at the same time built her sister ship the *Hibernia*, and the two vessels were launched on the same day off the Greenhithe yard in 1906. The two barges were identical and it was difficult to tell one from the other.

116

The *Cambria* is a beautiful model and is, in my opinion, the 'showiest' and best looking of all sailing barges. She has made fast passages with a consistent regularity for years and years and has won races in the days when there was a class for the big coasters. She carries 170 tons of cargo manfully — the same as the old *Greenhithe*, but without the same amount of deck water to go with it! She sets the biggest topsail out of London River and is more weatherly and handier than my old *Greenhithe* ever knew how to be. My old ship had never been fully repaired and was put to serve as a houseboat for night-working lightermen at the Tunnel Cement wharf in Long Reach, from which she had loaded so many freights in the past.

When I joined the *Cambria*, Alf Naylor, the company's sailmaker, was making her a complete new suit of sails, and although we had to bend them in winter weather and stretch them to shape in rain, gales and snow blizzards, they stood handsomely and earned a deal of praise when she sailed in the annual races.

For a mate I had Billy Evans, who had spent some eight years of his young life as mate of the *Cambria* under Capt Frank Tovell ('Cully' to all the coasting fraternity). Billy was a sound mate and knew his job, and being also a conscientious chap, was up to the high standard of mates I had always insisted on in the past. He said little and worked well.

Soon we were busy getting her into better trim than she had been, trading the winter months to Ipswich, Norwich and Yarmouth. For me it was pleasant to tread a wooden deck again and know the comfort of a wooden ship's cabin. I decided she was the best and most comfortable ship I had been in, with the possible exception of the old boom-rigged *Martinet*, which had become a war casualty in 1941. She was fast for her size and would snore to windward in heavy weather even without a topsail on her.

After a winter's trading, the firm decided to put her in the barge races against the two 'flyers' *Sara* and *Sirdar*, and although she was not expected to stand much chance unless there came an unholy gale of wind, there was no doubt that she was the finest looking craft of the day.

She was on the slipway for six weeks getting ready for the two traditional races — the Thames and Medway — and all our wire and running rigging, with the exception of the main shrouds, was renewed. She needed this refit anyway as it had been a long time since she had been commanded by anyone interested in hustling her along. Her mis-shapen old leeboards were put ashore and a new pair made, twenty-one feet six inches long and with a nine foot 'fan.' In the week of trials before the racing the *Cambria* showed up well against the *Sara*, but only because it was a week of strong, squally winds; and it was obvious that in a day's racing the *Sara* would have the measure of us.

I had as mainsheetman my old friend Tom Willis, a 'born and bred' bargeman who had been forced to leave the 280 ton *Ethel Everard* on the beach at Dunkirk in the course of the historic evacuation of British troops in 1940. Since then he had been master of motor ships and was allowed leave from the 700 tons *Sonority* to come and sail with me in the races. The forward hands comprised the mate Billy Evans, Chris Alston, who had become a rigger-sailmaker after being injured when mate of his father's barge, and Albert Day, son of old skipper Frank Day who had been master of the *Will Everard* and *Martha* for so many years. Albert had served with his father in these barges and been brought up in the old tradition; and a smarter and more enthusiastic jibsheetman no skipper could ever wish to have.

On the day before the race we sailed down to Gravesend for inspection by the race committee and saw the London and Rochester Company's *Sirdar* arrive in tow of one of their tugs. Painted a golden brown, low sided and her paintwork as smooth as glass, with a bowsprit nearly as long as her mainmast, she looked a proper flyer, more like a yacht than a Thames barge. She wore her sails white instead of having them dressed in the traditional red. She had done no work for something like two years, being kept for racing only. The *Sara* looked well, too, and as champion was favourite for the race, but Tommy Willis remarked to me as we eyed the Rochester barge 'She's going to take some catching.' He was right.

The great day was all against us in the *Cambria*. It was fine and sunny with a light summer breeze from a bit to the north of west. *Sara* got a good start and led the way out to the mark at the North Oaze buoy, *Sirdar* some three hundred yards astern of her and *Cambria* about the same distance behind the *Sirdar*. Near the mark both the other barges took in their spinnakers early and trimmed on the wind, but by holding on to our running canvas longer and dropping it all in smartly almost on top of the buoy we gained a good deal on the *Sirdar* and incidentally won for ourselves the Royal London Yacht Club's silver medal for the best seamanship.

As *Cambria* came on the wind with a big two-sheeted jib set we prayed for a freshening breeze. But instead it fell away to a calm and, restricted by the rules to five sails and not allowed a light foresail, we were left floundering and creeping along at about two knots while the two flyers ghosted away from us and engaged in a battle of wits as the flood came off Southend. Sailed freer than the *Sara*, the *Sirdar* overhauled the champion and went gliding through her lee. Tack and tack, in paltry airs, the two fought it out, sometimes one ahead and sometimes the other, but all the time the *Sirdar* was travelling that little bit faster. By the time they reached the Lower Hope she had a winning lead and the *Sara* could not catch her as she hauled into Gravesend Reach to the accompaniment of every ship's siren on the river — a new champion at last.

In the Medway race the wind was easterly, fresh enough to kick up a few white horses outside Sheerness. *Cambria* made a good start this time but in the short turns to windward in the narrow Medway the two little flyers were able to make a complete board across the river while we were coming about. Once more the *Sirdar* outpaced the *Sara*, more convincingly this time, but on the run home the old *Cambria*, spreading her wings, actually beat the champion's time from the mark to the finish by four minutes. But this was not enough to make up the time we had lost in the turn to windward. The racing over, the *Sara* and *Sirdar* returned to the respective yards to be put back into 'moth balls' while the old *Cambria* sailed away to load palm kernels at Felixstowe Dock for Erith — the only genuine working barge in the race. Within a fortnight we had delivered two of these cargoes and were then ordered to Millwall Dock to load wheat for Norwich.

That was the last match sailing the *Cambria* took part in though there is always the possibility that she might try again after this book has been published. In subsequent years I raced in the *Sara*, and later rigged out the old *Dreadnought* to win the Thames championship in the Staysail Class. In fact, at the time of writing I have the honour to be master of two barges, *Cambria* for working and *Dreadnought* for racing. And I'm very proud of both of them.

Slow Passage

———— ❋ ————

THE Millwall Dock is no place for a barge to go if the crew take any pride in her appearance. Great chunks of our lovely racing paint and goldleaf scroll work were chafed and scraped unmercifully by dumb lighters (and 'dumb' lightermen) and after our brief visit there to load at the Central Granary we lost our 'shine' and began to look much more like a workaday barge.

It was one of those passages which would make any bargeman swear. After loading and later getting in stores at Greenhithe, we got under way with fickle airs from the north-west, falling to a calm as we sidled down Northfleet Hope. Little puffs and catspaws came and went and there was some anchor drill in Gravesend Reach to keep her from being set too far into Northfleet bight. After a morning's heaving and sweating (and swearing) we only got as far as Chapman Head (about fourteen miles) when the anchor had to go down to hold her against the oncoming flood tide. The next ebb, in the evening, ran so sluggishly that with the paltry head winds we met we only got down as far as the South-East Maplin, another eighteen miles. Down went the anchor again at low water and we laid off the sand edge until the next early morning ebb which, running no faster than the previous day and accompanied by changeable airs, took us down as far as the Gunfleet Spit in the East Swin

Channel. This was a bit better progress and a gentle westerly wind came so that we could keep under way against the flood. But even this favourable slant died away on the night ebb and by low water at one o'clock in the morning we had failed to round Orfordness and had to anchor off the Whiting Sand.

Bill said: 'We'll take a ruddy week to get there at this rate,' and remarked that of all the years he had spent in the *Cambria* this was the longest drift down he had ever had in her.

I was on deck at crack of day but to my dismay the rising sun was blotted out by thick fog. All round us was a blanket of white, soaking the sails and dripping dolefully off the rigging, reducing visibility to about 100 feet. Bill and I ate our breakfast gloomily and then as the ebb came away with a faint suspicion of a breeze from the north-east (right ahead) we drifted and sailed 'blindfold' round Ordfordness, casting the lead now and then and listening for the rattle of shingle in the lazy swell onshore. After three hours of this the heat of the sun broke up the fog and there was Thorpeness close under our lee. Another tide almost wasted — and then came a smart breeze from the worst possible direction — north-east. In sheets, down leeboard, and the old barge stood off the land as the shallow swell got up.

All the next flood I was compelled to keep under way, slashing to windward against a rising, awkward sea. We made hardly any progress, less than three miles, in the whole of the adverse tide, but with the wind on the land there was no place to bring up without running back round Orfordness into Hollesley Bay. And that I would not do with the prospect of a fine night. It was only an afternoon breeze such as one frequently gets in summer time, but it blew quite fresh for a few hours.

That evening, as the ebb started, the sea went down, the wind fell and we gently turned past Southwold, hauling inside the Barnard Sand as the breeze shifted to the north-west, so that we could keep in the Covehithe Channel close under the sand dunes and cliffs where there is a narrow deep water channel (deep for a barge, anyway). But no sooner did Bill and I start estimating what time we should arrive in Yarmouth harbour, than the shore, close aboard by now, was suddenly blotted out completely by thick fog. It was dark, too, and not a light could we see.

The breeze held from about north-north-west and with the lead line going we groped our way to windward between the Inner Shoal and Lowestoft. Once or twice the lights on the cliff top glimmered uncomfortably near up above us and we winded hastily, losing sight of them immediately. Once a motor car hooted continuously as we came about under Lowestoft and I thought that the driver must have been a seaman and seeing our masts was trying to warn us how near the shore we were.

Eventually, not without a deal of anxiety, we found the tide rip off Lowestoft Ness, which to a coasting sailor is as good as any buoy or beacon, and were able to stand off a little further into the deeper water of the North Road. By this time the fog was so thick that it was not safe to keep turning to windward through the roadstead. Apart from the danger of running ashore on the westward tack, there were probably several ships or trawlers at anchor which we would not be able to see in time to keep clear of collision.

So down the anchor had to go, even though the tide would have set us nearly to our destination.

Bill, never a talkative chap, said a couple of crisp words (quite unprintable) which adequately summed up our feelings, and pulled up the riding light. It was past midnight and we lay in our bunks until just before the break of day. But the fog was still with us though there was a moderate northerly breeze.

We brewed tea and sat on the main horse hoping for a sight of the shore or perhaps the West Holm buoy. Suddenly, as so often happens in fog, the blanket lifted for

a matter of two or three minutes. There was the buoy some
hundred yards away. We could see the shore and only one
vessel — a fisherman — at anchor in the roads. Although
the fog closed down again I had seen enough to get under
way. Up anchor, and we once more tacked slowly northwards, peering through the now thinning mist for a sight
of Yarmouth pierheads or Goreleston Cliff.

At last the sun broke through and the fog disappeared as
if by magic. There we were within a couple of boards of
the south pierhead. The wind was too far out of the harbour
entrance to sail in over the ebb so we hoisted Y.A. on our
flag halliards and jilled her about until the harbour tug —
the *Richard Lee Barber* — came out to tow us in.

'Hello Bob,' called Sam, the tug skipper. 'Where you
for?'

'The blasted lunatic asylum' I answered, 'if we have any
more weather like this.'

We had taken four days to make a 120 miles passage.

But the *Cambria* is no slow-coach when she feels a decent
breeze. One winter's night we mustered from Greenhithe,
bound to Norwich with wheat, just as darkness was closing
in. There was a strong south-west wind which had been
blowing for several days; not a gale, but rough and blustery.
By the time we were down Sea Reach several cloths of the
mainsail had to be brailed up to ease the helm and she
streaked off down the West and East Swin channels with a
wake like a packet boat. Before daylight we were off
Yarmouth pierheads, having run 114 miles in exactly
fifteen hours, the fastest I had ever sailed that particular
passage fully loaded.

Pleased and proud at having made a record run we were
soon reminded that there is always some hitch or setback
in every little triumph or accomplishment. Nothing ever
goes right *all* the time. Soon there was a morse lamp
flashing from the South Pier and laboriously I spelt out
the signal while the mate held the wheel.

'No — tug — until — Monday.' And this was Friday!

To make matters worse the southerly gale cone was being hoisted ashore and the B.B.C. interrupted their early morning music with those ominous words: 'Here is a gale warning. South to south-west gale imminent in Humber, Thames and Dover — .'

There was quite enough wind and sea already, but too far south-westerly for us to fetch into the harbour under sail. Either we had to get in on our own (and Yarmouth is one of the worst harbours on the East Coast to take without a leading wind) or else run on northwards in order to find a weather shore for shelter along by Haisborough. And if we did that Heaven knows how long we should be getting back south to Yarmouth again — a pretty end to what we had been proud to call a record run!

The harbour tug (so it transpired) was in dry dock and although the Haven Commissioners claimed a monopoly of towage no provision of any sort had been made to cover the period during which the tug was laid up.

I had as mate with me at the time a young Kentish lad (or was he a Lad of Kent?), Nobby Lambkin, whose father had been a Medway bargeman of the old school and told his son to 'Get to sea in a barge and learn something about the job before you go in a motor ship.' Nobby had been third hand when I first took the *Cambria* and now he had come back as mate when Bill Evans (after eleven years mate of the *Cambria*) finally settled down to married life and a shipyard job. Nobby was only seventeen but he was as broad and strong as a full grown man. We also had with us on that trip a young student who had to be back at his university on Monday morning and he looked a bit crestfallen when I told him of the message from the pierhead.

Nobby looked at me and I think he knew what I had in mind.

'She's got to go in, Nob. Get everything set smart.'

We jilled around until we saw the flood tide coming up through the roads. From a suitable offing I put her on the port tack and let the tide soak her up along the land so that as we came close to the entrance she had to bear up and thus pick up greater and greater speed as we went surging for the north pier. As we came into the tidal shoot from inside the south pier I down-helm and shook her up head to wind.

I had told Nobby that on no account was she to fill her foresail on the starboard tack. He had a line rove through the bowline cringle and stood facing aft, watching me and ready for anything. As the barge began to lose way with her sails ashake I called out 'Back her' . . .

Nobby and the student hauled the heavy foresail aweather and the *Cambria* paid off on the port tack again, once more threatening to knock her head in as she charged at the north pier.

Down-helm again: but she was slow to answer now and she would not luff clear of the inner end of the north pier.

'Down foresail.' The pressure off her head, she edged, hesitatingly, into the wind again. The sluicing flood swept her past the piles with a yard to spare. We were round the corner.

'Up foresail; haul her aback.'

Nobby was heaving and sweating, and swearing at the student, but to my relief he got the heavy foresail up and aweather again in time. Slowly she boxed round as she was set swiftly athwart the tide and bore away with her head pointing up the harbour. We'd done it. We were in.

A harbour official shouted something about the tug — Nobby told him what he could do with it — *Cambria* didn't need one now.

While I had Nobby as mate in the *Cambria* we made some fast passages (and some rough ones) running between the Humber and Margate. Our best was when we left Spurn Head at six o'clock in the morning, were in Yarmouth

126

Roads that night and off the Kentish Knock the next daylight. Then we were becalmed for several hours with only fitful catspaws to keep us off the sand; and that spoilt a fine run. The worst thing about running to Margate is that the best wind from the Humber is a north-wester but that gives you a bad lee shore to run for at Margate; and a bad harbour in the bargain which can only be taken near high water because it dries out on the ebb. More than one sailing barge has arrived off Margate with coal from the North, taken one look at the harbour entrance and finished up sheltering (if you can call it shelter) under the Hook Sand or even in the Medway.

When Nobby left — to marry and raise a family — mates were hard to come by. The old sea breed seemed to be dying out with the changing times. I had to take on people unsuited to the job and the life it entailed — college lads, landsmen and amusement crazy youths whose outlook seemed shallow and meaningless. Like the barge, I had not moved with the times — they liked noise, excitement and queer exotic clothes. And the waterside pubs were wracked with juke boxes whereby a single youth with a threepenny piece could kill all conversation and friendly meetings.

Third hands were out of the question. Young lads did not want to go to sea in a sailing barge because they said: (1) there was no future in it; (2) it was just a lot of hard work; (3) they did not like going aloft; (4) there was not enough money in it; (5) the hours were too long; (6) they never knew when they were going to get ashore; (7) and it was too lonely. So the best we could do for a third hand was a cunning old lurcher bitch named Dusty who used to keep off intruders in port, kill rats, scrounge meals off neighbouring ships and occupy my bunk during bad weather at sea. Perhaps her worst habit was that as soon as we came in from sea and got alongside she would leap ashore straight into the nearest pub as though she knew that the master would surely follow.

ACCOMODATION FOR MASTER

A Maldon skipper once took his wife's pet dog for a trip to London in his barge while the good lady was away visiting relatives. He had strict instructions as to the care and maintenance of the animal and it was more than his life was worth that it should come to any harm. Another Maldon skipper, his bitter rival, knew about this and the two of them sailed for London on the same tide. Both loaded in the Surrey Dock, each keeping a wary eye on the other, each determined to be the first barge to get back to Maldon. At last both were loaded and ready to lock out on the early morning tide, there being a splendid south-west breeze blowing, which would give them a good run to the River Blackwater.

The little dog, having been put on deck to do his duty while master and mate had their breakfast, noticed a man from the other barge offering him tasty morsels of meat. The precious animal nimbly skipped aboard the rival craft, only to be roughly collared by a pair of horny hands and unceremoniously bundled down the forecastle and locked in — albeit with a fine feed of bits and bones to keep him quiet.

Soon the lock foreman's voice was heard; 'Sailorman, ahoy. Let 'em come.'

One barge was hove smartly into the lock but the other hung back.

'Your other barge coming out?'

'Dunno. Lorst his dawg or somethin'.'

Whistles and calls were heard from behind the warehouses and presently a somewhat distracted barge skipper appeared at the lockside.

'How long can you hang on for us. I've lost my missus' little old dawg. He was aboard a few minutes ago. Can't be far away. Little white dawg.'

'I can't wait any longer this lock,' said the P.L.A. official. 'We shall be locking out again in about two hours. Perhaps you'll have found him by then.'

Needless to say, the search went on all day and the barge remained moored to the quay while his rival was bowling away down Sea Reach, enjoying the best of a fair wind and tide and her crew relieved of the anxiety of having to race against a faster rival. Meantime two weary bargemen trod almost every inch of the Surrey Dock, searched every warehouse, and explored half of Rotherhithe. And it was not until the following day that, gloomy and downhearted, they locked out and sailed away for Maldon, beset, as bad luck would have it, by light headwinds and calms. By the time they arrived in Maldon the other barge had finished unloading and was getting ready to come away again. And the jibes and comments about fast passages, losing fair winds and keeping your eyes skinned were not easy to bear. But for the skipper there was worse to come.

His rival, on reaching Maldon, had released the dog, who, immediately recognising his native soil, bolted up the road for home, to be welcomed by his mistress who had returned from her holiday. Assuming that the skipper could not be far away she bustled round to prepare him a hot dinner.

It was three days before he showed his face at the door, to get what married men call 'a cold dinner and a warm reception'. Without any chance to get a word in edgeways, he was angrily accused of wasting his time in the local pub and sleeping aboard the barge instead of coming home. 'It's no good you telling me you've only just arrived. I know very well your barge has been in the port this last three days because the dog's been home.' And so on and so on.

Mystified, the old skipper sat down in silence and took it all on his broad shoulders. Some two years later he told me a tale of how he once had a dog aboard which found its way home to Maldon from the Surrey Dock and got there quicker than the barge. Another year went by before I learned the facts from the mate of the other barge, thus revealing to me the story as I have set it down here. To the day of his death I do not believe the skipper who lost the dog ever knew how the animal found its way home.

This is only one of the classic old tales which one could always hear among the barging fraternity. There was another, attributed to more than one skipper, about a barge in thick fog edging down along the Shoebury Sands past the Admiralty Beacons, and a somewhat stupid mate being sent forward to look for the Blacktail Spit buoy. Presently he called out: 'I can see something, skipper.'

'What is it? A big black buoy with a knob on it?'

'No skipper. It's a man on a horse.'

'Bloody fool! Man on a horse! That's the Blacktail Spit buoy, you ruddy dunderhead. Here, come and hold on to this wheel and let me see how she bears.'

The skipper went forward and after a few moments came aft again looking somewhat shaken. He looked solemnly at his mate and said: 'I'm getting as bad as you. We're both bloody nuts. I've had you here too long. It *is* a man on a

Early muster

horse; swimming about in the sea. Look there he comes. Chuck him that heaving line.'

So the barge was put alongside the horse, its rider taken off and the horse hove aboard on the burton tackle, put down in the main hold and tethered to the main beam, to be finally unloaded at Felixstowe Dock. Other versions of the tale say the horse was drowned in the process. But the main part of the story is quite true, for the rider was an Army officer from Shoebury artillery base who had gone out riding over the sands at low water, got lost in the fog and been cut off by the flood tide.

Wherever bargemen foregathered, sitting on someone's main-horse or hatches in summer weather or harvesting pints in a harbour pub, there was always a yarn to be told, some of them year after year and never losing their flavour. Jack Josh, the tough old Gravesend skipper, used to tell us how he was lying in Margate Roads in the First World War and the Germans came and took him out of her. He and his mate finished up in a prisoner of war camp in Germany. 'When the soldiers asked me where I was captured I said "England"; and they wouldn't believe me!' There were stories of tragedy too; of men being drowned on winter nights and frozen bodies in the topsail of a sunken barge. They were all tales worth listening to. And they were true. A reflection of the life and character of the men who told them.

Farewell to Sailormen

———— ❦ ————

THERE is not a happy ending to this book. The last chapter must needs be a sad one because as I write the last of the sailormen, both craft and crews, are fading peacefully into the past. Of the coasters there is only the *Cambria* left. For companions as far as Harwich she has the *Anglia* and *Marjorie*, still occasionally carrying grain and cattle feed for their owners, R. & W. Paul of Ipswich. But London to Ipswich is their one and only run. Even less frequently in cargo are three barges belonging to Cranfields, the Ipswich millers — the *Spinaway C*, *Venture* and *May;* but lack of experienced crews brings their eclipse uncomfortably near, though one or two young Ipswich lads have made praiseworthy efforts to keep them in commission.

The extinction of the sailing barge does not only mean the loss of a unique and picturesque type of sailing vessel, but also the extinction of the type of man who sailed in her. Because of the nature of his employment he was strongly individualistic, bold, intelligent and independent.

The breed has almost died out now. These men knew the pleasanter side of life, too, and most of them had an appreciation of quietness and beauty. What better for a man's peace of mind than to sit on the main-horse of a barge anchored in a quiet creek and hear the tinkle of the tide round the leeboards, listen to the sandpipers and curlews on the flats and ruminate on the possibilities of tomorrow's weather.

Gone, too, are the old 'guv'nors', men of enterprise and hard work who owned and operated these barges. Many 'guv'nors' started life as a bargeman themselves, or perhaps as barge builders. They called a spade a spade, trusted their bargemasters, and knew them far better than employers in the modern coasting trade of engines, unions, rules and time schedules. And the bargemen knew them. Each held the other in a friendly respect which I have never known in any other trade or industry (except perhaps farming). The older bargemen were very loyal to their guv'nors and used to stick up for them stoutly in all sorts of ways. To sail for a bad guv'nor was a reflection on himself so he generally gave of his best to the man he had chosen to work for.

But as the old guv'nors faded away the bargemen could not understand the ways of the people with whom he was left to deal. They were not of his world. They knew nothing of his ways; less of his character; and little of his barge. The bargeman had always sailed for a guv'nor he knew — not for some vague office organisation which he did not feel inclined to try and understand. For this reason many packed up while there were still sailing barges to earn a living in.

This book is really a farewell to them all. Their age is past. Their old art and skill is already being lost and the standard of seamanship in the new race of motorised bargemen is visibly dropping. No more will there be skippers and mates with such a rich knowledge of the winds and tides who can handle vessels under sail in narrow waters and in fierce running tides and yet face the open sea with equal confidence and skill. In gales, calms or fogs the sailorman always had something up his sleeve — some ancient manoeuvre from forgotten days, some cunning trick handed down by skippers long dead; or perhaps some daring dodge of their own evolved through the hard years of training. They were never at a loss to know what to do.

Accustomed to long hours, hard times and adversity, they
rode over so many obstacles in the course of their daily
calling that they developed a hardy character and cheerful
outlook that refused to be dismayed by anything.

Twin screws and diesel oil do not breed the 'characters'
who became known from the Humber to the Isle of Wight,
whose names were household words among the coasting
fraternity — beholden to no man, and confident in their
ability as bargemen, and proud of their calling. Like
Chaucer's 'shipman' of eight hundred years ago.

> Hardy he was and wise to undertake;
> With many a tempest had his beard been shake.
> He knew well all the havens as they were,
> From Scotland to the Cape of Finisterre,
> And every creek in Britain and in Spain;
> His barge was named the 'Magdelayne'.'

The few surviving barges have now become objects of
curiosity and the *Cambria* is probably the most photographed
vessel on the English coast. The mate and I are pointed out
ashore (sometimes with pity) as 'these blokes without an
engine'. Of course we get asked a host of stupid questions,
which reminds me of a day in a Suffolk riverside inn when
I was having a quiet pint with an old skipper. A bus load
of trippers arrived and inquiring of the landlord about
'those funny old boats off there,' they were told that the two
skippers were over in the corner. We were immediately
surrounded and bombarded with such questions as 'Do
you anchor at night?' 'What do you do when the wind is
against you?' 'How long does it take you to get to London?'
'Why don't you have engines put in?' etc., etc.

We answered as best we could for the landlord's sake
but as they thinned away I remarked to my old friend, 'Half
the people ashore seem to be as ignorant as Hell.' To which
he quickly replied. 'Ah, that they are: they're bloody near
as ignorant as the other half.' And he drank his ale with an

Down below

air of contempt and departed, because he had heard a curlew on the mudflat and knew that it was half ebb and time for his barge to be under way.

So comes the end of my story. There does not seem to be anything else to write about barges. The last of the sailormen is still at work, perhaps for another five years, maybe ten — or even more. The *Cambria* is no longer an ordinary work-a-day coaster fitting in unnoticed with London River's busy scene. She has become something for people to stare at. Steamboatmen call each other out of their quarters to come and look at us as they rattle by. We see binoculars trained on us from liners' bridges, and from Navy ships, too. Scandinavian seamen, having a closer link with sail than the British, invariably give us a friendly wave. Passengers train their cameras on us. An American even came across the Atlantic to have a sail in the *Cambria* while there was still a spritty left and hustled off home with seventy-three photographs of the barge and her gear.

Perhaps it is fitting then that I write these last few lines in the *Cambria's* cabin while she is under way, the mate at the wheel, heading seaward past the Nore. In her hold is a cargo of bran for Yarmouth. From there she is bound north to the Humber and Trent to load 170 tons of coal for Margate. Her bowsprit down and two jibs set, all her canvas is drawing to a freshening westerly breeze and the smooth water chatters by as she makes a comfortable seven knots. Coming down London River a big Gravesend tug gave us a 'cocka-doodle-doo' on his whistle and I daresay the old barge justified the compliment as she heeled to the breeze, her gilt scrolls and varnished spars bright in the mid-day sun.

The last of the sailormen indeed, but not yet, not quite yet, a thing of the past.